MY EAR AT HIS HEART

by the same author

plays
PLAYS ONE
(*The King and Me, Outskirts, Borderline, Birds of Passage*)
SLEEP WITH ME
WHEN THE NIGHT BEGINS

screenplays
MY BEAUTIFUL LAUNDRETTE & OTHER WRITINGS
SAMMY AND ROSIE GET LAID
LONDON KILLS ME
MY SON THE FANATIC
THE MOTHER
COLLECTED SCREENPLAYS I

fiction
THE BUDDHA OF SUBURBIA
THE BLACK ALBUM
LOVE IN A BLUE TIME
INTIMACY
MIDNIGHT ALL DAY
GABRIEL'S GIFT
THE BODY AND OTHER STORIES

non-fiction
THE FABER BOOK OF POP (edited with Jon Savage)
DREAMING AND SCHEMING

My Ear at His Heart

Reading My Father

HANIF KUREISHI

faber and faber

First published in 2004
by Faber and Faber Limited
3 Queen Square London WC1N 3AU

Typeset by Faber and Faber Limited
Printed in England by Mackays of Chatham plc,
Chatham, Kent

A CIP record for this book
is available from the British Library

ISBN 0-571-22403-2

2 4 6 8 10 9 7 5 3 1

For my mother, and for my sons

CHAPTER ONE

On the floor in a corner of my study, sticking out from under a pile of other papers, is a shabby old green folder containing a manuscript I believe will tell me a lot about my father and my own past. But ever since it was discovered I have been glancing at it, looking away, getting on with something else, thinking about it, doing nothing. The manuscript was given to me a few weeks ago, having turned up after more than eleven years. It is a novel written by my father, a legacy of words, a protracted will, perhaps – I don't know yet what it contains. Like all his fiction it was never published. I think I should read it.

When I first conceived the book I am now writing, lying in bed at night – before the discovery of dad's text – I intended it to start with other books. I was wondering about the past as I often do now, dreaming further and further back, and thought that a way of capturing the flavour of my younger self might be to reread the writers I'd liked as a young man. I would look at, for instance, Kerouac, Dostoevsky, Salinger, Orwell, Hesse, Ian Fleming and Wilde again, in order to see whether I could rein-habit the worlds they once made in my head, and identify myself in them.

As well as being about the writers who'd meant most to me, the book would be about the 1960s and 70s, set alongside the present, with some material about the context in which the reading, and then the rereading, took place. Each book, I

1

hoped, would revive memories of the circumstances in which it was read. It would then set me thinking about what each particular book had come to mean for me.

Whoever else was in it, I decided right away that the focus would be Chekhov's work, his letters, plays and stories. He had been one of my father's favourite writers, a man and doctor we discussed often. All books contain some sort of attitude towards life, and most such approaches you grow out of; like dead relationships, they no longer offer you anything. But I am still curious about Chekhov and the numerous voices his work can sustain, and often think of returning not only to his writing, but to him as a man, to the way he thought and felt, and to the questions he asked.

I came to some sort of self- and political consciousness in the 1970s, a particularly ideological time of aggressive self-description. Women, gays and blacks were beginning to speak a new or undiscovered rendition of their history. If you wanted to work in the theatre, as I did, it was impossible to escape the argument that culture was inevitably political. When Trotsky wrote, 'The function of art in our epoch is determined by its attitude towards the revolution', the only questions for writers were: where did you stand? and, what were you doing? (You couldn't say, what revolution? without ruling yourself out of the conversation.)

When I didn't know what the purpose of my writing was, or when I wanted to think of what I did as an exploration of ideas and character, I'd remember Chekhov. He was a subtle writer, a supreme poet of disillusionment, suffering and stasis; and, like Albert Camus, a man who saw that being pushed into an ideological corner was of no benefit to anyone.

The book I intended originally to write would have a 'loose' form, being a journal rather than criticism, and be about the way one reads or uses literature, as much as anything else. After all, it is rare – rare for me – to read a book from beginning to end in one go. I read, live, return to a book, forget who the characters are (particularly if they have Russian names), pick up another book, put it down, go on holiday and, maybe, get to the end while having forgotten the beginning.

As an adolescent, and in my twenties and thirties, I read consistently and even seriously. By seriously I mean I read stuff I didn't want to read, even making notes, hoping this would help the material become part of me. I felt I'd had a pretty poor education until the age of sixteen. Or, rather, having read so many public-school novels – school novels then didn't seem to be any other kind – I had intimidating fantasies about those book-stuffed public-school boys, kids like my father, who knew Latin and understood syntax. I was convinced they'd be way ahead of me, intellectually and therefore socially. People would want to hear what they had to say.

What I required from reading was to extend my knowledge and what I thought of as my 'orientation'. This meant having new ideas, which would function like tools or instructions, making me feel less helpless in the world, less bereft, less of a child. If you knew about things in advance, they wouldn't seem so intimidating, you would be prepared, as though you'd been given a map of the future. My mother and sister mystified me, so I wanted, for instance, to find out about sex, and what women were like, what they felt and thought about, and whether it was different from men, particularly when men were not present. And, when I began writing myself, I wanted to find out what was going on in the literary arena, what other writers were thinking and doing – how they were symbolising the contemporary world, for instance – and what I, in turn, might be able to do.

Although I have this idea of myself as not having enough education – enough for what? – a couple of years ago my mother found, in the attic of our house in the suburbs where she still lives, a notebook with a home-made cover of wallpaper. I started it in 1964, when I was ten, and listed the books I had read. It must have been around then that I began to write everything down in an ever-increasing number of pompously-named notebooks, as though the world only had reality once it was translated into words. Thinking about this now, I can't help but find it odd that for me 'education' always meant reading, the accumulation of information. I never thought of it in terms of experience, for instance, or feeling or pleasure or conversation.

In 1964, to my surprise, I read one hundred and twenty-two books. Some Arthur Ransome; more than enough Enid Blyton; E. Nesbit; Mark Twain; Richmal Crompton; oddities like *Pakistan Cricket on the March*; *Adventure Stories for Boys* by 'lots and lots of people'; *Stalky & Co* and *The Jungle Book*.

Four years later, in 1968, the tone had changed. January begins with *Billy Bunter the Hiker* but right after it came *The Man with the Golden Gun*, which is followed by *G-Man at the Yard* by Peter Cheyney. Then it's *From Russia With Love*, *The Saint*, *The Freddie Trueman Story*, P. G. Wodehouse, Mickey Spillane, and the Beatles biography by Hunter Davies (in brackets, 're-read', which is unusual for me at that stage). Finally there is *Writing and Selling Fact & Fiction* by Harry Edward Neal.

4

In 1974 I was supposed to be at university, but didn't feel like attending classes. After all, I'd been at school, sitting still and listening, since I was five. I was, in fact, writing and living with my girlfriend in Morecambe, Lancashire, a run-down freezing seaside town not far from the Heysham Head nuclear power station. It was the first time I'd lived with anyone not my parents. Once we hitch-hiked to the Lake District, otherwise we'd walk on the cliffs and the sand, and listen to music. Sometimes we would cook and eat huge meals, consisting of five or six courses, eating until we were stuffed, until we couldn't move, and passed out where we lay.

Morecambe was far from London. That was the idea. Except that you leave home and recreate your home life in another place, where the regime you make is even more fervent, the obedience greater. I was, therefore, mostly behind a closed door, having written in my diary, in 1970, 'The idea is for me to stay in my room all the time.' This was my father's wish for me – one he made when he thought I should become a writer – and it was already the only place I felt safe, something I would feel for years, and still do, to a certain extent. Perhaps my girlfriend made me embarrassed about the writing-things-down habit, as well as the lists, notebooks and much else. (I still do the lists, but about other things.) The books read during this time are by Sartre and Camus, Alan Watts and Beckett, before the lists stop. Maybe, for a bit, I went out into the world. The last entry is Fitzgerald's *The Beautiful and Damned*, of which I recall almost nothing, only the memorable image of a weeping woman on a bed, half-mad, embracing a shoe. I liked anything erotic, of course. Not that there had been much around. *Lady Chatterley*, *Lolita* and even *The Catcher in the Rye* – then considered to be a 'dirty' book – were kept in dad's bedroom. None of them did much for me. James Bond was better; Harold Robbins represented a delicious, shameless indulgence. My girlfriend, who was a good teacher, introduced me to the work of Philip Roth and Erica Jong, as well as to that of Miles Davis and Mahler.

But these are other artists and I am vacillating. Pressingly, there is still the question of the semi-hidden book in the folder poking out from under a pile of other papers in my study, papers I have yet to find a place for, which reproach me every time I spot them. I have to say that I know the folder contains a novel called 'An Indian Adolescence'. My father, who was a civil servant in the Pakistan Embassy in London, wrote novels, stories, and stage and radio plays all his adult life. I think he completed at least four novels, though all were turned down by numerous publishers and agents, which was traumatic for our family, who took the rejection personally. But dad did publish journalism about Pakistan, and about squash and cricket, and wrote two books on Pakistan for young people.

I am sure that 'An Indian Adolescence' was his last novel, written, I guess, after his heart surgery, a bypass, when he was no longer employed in the Embassy, where he'd worked most of his adult life. I have little idea what to expect from dad's novel, but I do anticipate being shocked and, probably, moved and disturbed. Will it be dreadful, a masterpiece, or something in between? Will it tell me a little, too much, or just the right amount? Why hesitate now? I wonder whether it will contain some sort of message to me, and how I might respond.

My father and his numerous brothers always read a lot, and seriously too. When they met, while cleaning and smoking their pipes, they'd talk about literature and politics, and swap books.

6

I guess knowledge was a competitive thing with them; they loved to argue, the intellectual tension between them was always high, almost murderous, as though they were wrestling. With my father there were Saturday trips to the 'book road' – Charing Cross Road – just the men, while my mother took my sister to her ballet class. The city itself was a revelation and a hope for this skinny little light-brown kid crossing the river on the train, passing through the slums of Herne Hill and Brixton from the suburbs. It was intimidating, a grand imperial metropolis full of massive statues: blank-faced men covered in bird-shit and medals, who had commanded armies and ruled nations. That was the Empire for me: decline, and these relics. It wasn't that for my father, who had lived in it, as I was beginning to understand when he spoke of his childhood – an incident with a brother or teacher here, a joke there, and nothing to make either of us sad.

Children hear scores of stories, in numerous forms, before they can read them. But at the centre of their education is their induction into an ongoing story. This is the family legend or tra- dition, various versions of which their parents and family are keen to impress on them. Whatever else was going on in my life, through books I was entering a narrative, or myth, which con- cerned reading, and writers, as a kind of family transaction. Sport – and cricket in particular – was part of this myth. Probably none of us would have been able to say exactly what sort of story it was. Nonetheless, an important communication was being made about what counted in the family, about how I should live and who I should be. If every child has their place in the family dream or economy, and the parents have a project for the child, neither they nor the child can be sure what it is.

By the time I'd left home, I'd come, unsurprisingly, to have great faith in books. Although father's blind spots in reading are mine, and what he disliked I still dislike – there's nothing as permanent as an inherited childhood phobia – I knew you could find a book for every mood, or find a book to change your mood, a book which might suggest a way of thinking, feeling and being. New thoughts, images and fantasies would spring into your mind as you sat reading. The right book, drug-like, could put you, and keep you, in the desired frame of mind for weeks.

After leaving London University, where I'd gone after only a year in the North, I was trying to be a writer, according to my father's plan. If I wrote in the morning, I'd walk around the city in the afternoon. It was aimless, I was a *flaneur* – a 'loafer' in father's words, meaning idler – getting to know London by its streets and faces, wishing I had someone to talk to, a girl to be with, and visiting second-hand bookshops, of which there were more than there are now, where you could always find odd things. I was probably more than slightly depressed. Out of curiosity I had started, once a week, to visit an old-fashioned mental asylum in Surrey where I was shocked to see drugged, shaven-headed lunatics jibbering in the corridors, and one old man who always wore a tutu. These trips were, purportedly, to provide the inmates with contact from the outside world, but I needed to find out about mental distress from more than a book. How mad was I? The supervisor allocated me the position of 'friend' to a porcelain-skinned German beauty who lived in the millionaires' square, the Boltons, in South Kensington. She was almost paralysed, like one of Freud's early cases, reminding me of a line by Anne Carson, '. . . the nerves pouring around in her like a palace fire.' Both her parents had killed themselves recently, one by jumping out of the window. We'd sit in her flat, watching the curtains rustle in the breeze; sometimes, drily, we'd kiss. She did her best, but she couldn't cheer me up.

I guess I was beginning to see that while you can't be subject to a book's will, neither will it kiss you, talk back or bring you a cup of tea. You begin to feel hungry and deprived, though you don't know what for, because you've been told that stories can give you so much. Surely they can cure both loneliness and the difficult reality of actual others?

The book trips I would make soon came to be the same every day. That was the point. In similar fashion, at the moment, although I'm not writing much, I've been coming into my study and sitting here as if I am working on something. The place I write is a room on the first floor of my house in West London, where I have two old computers and am surrounded by books, CDs, photographs and children's drawings, as well as a drawing of dad by my mother. I have dozens of pens nearby, many of them fountain pens – which I enjoy washing and filling – some of which belonged to my father. I prefer to write by hand rather than type; the movement of the arm seems closer to drawing – doodling, rather – and to inner movement. Ultimately these are habits; daily repetitions. A new thing is an excuse for another thing the same. Then you know where you are. Beckett is full of these obsessions – you might call his an aesthetic of futile repetitions.

Don't think I haven't noticed that many artists are as compelled by the rituals which surround their art – silence, covering paper, screwing it up, tossing it in the bin – as much as by the matter itself. After a few years it becomes obvious that the art is there to serve the ritual, which is everything. If you aren't an obsessive, you can't be an artist, however imaginative you might be. Yet, sometimes, I think I go to my desk only to obey my father. This might explain why I'm so furious when I arrive there and why I don't know what to do when I'm finished. Yet if that was all there was to it, I'd have found another profession by now.

Now, embarked on this 'reading' project and thinking I really ought to get on with it, I take the manuscript from its folder and flick through it. Holding onto the book for a while before replacing it, I continue to wonder what I should do with this object, or gift, made by dad. It is like a letter from the dead, delivered more than ten years late. Yet however long it has been unread, I suppose a book becomes a real book if even just one person opens it and tries to receive its communication. Looking at the inaccurate typing, crossings-out and scribbled additions of this one makes me think of the limitations of the mass-produced novel with its impression of impersonality, objectivity and authority. Sometimes I fancy making my own books, handwritten in different colours, including photographs, drawings and alternative versions, which would give an impression of its making or process.

I am wary of forgetting the conditions under which my father wrote. He was ill for most of my adolescence. He was either in hospital, or recuperating, or about to go back to work, or getting ill again. His father was an Army doctor who wanted his sons and daughters to train as doctors. Oddly, none did; though dad made sure he got to spend a lot of time with doctors, as well as with – via the local library – Zen masters and Buddhists of various types, and literary 'soul-doctors' like Jung and Alan Watts.

In place of a discarded Islam, and functioning like spiritual medicine, dad – a Muslim who had left India in his early twenties and never returned – made a religion at home out of library books, discontent and literary ambition. It must have been cheering for him to know he wasn't the only suburban mystic. Alan Watts had been born a bus ride away, in Chislehurst; he'd been to school in nearby Bickley, before going to King's School, Canterbury, which the other doctor-writer, Somerset Maugham, had attended, writing about it in *Of Human Bondage*. Watts then moved to Bromley.

It was partly through Watts, who occasionally appeared on TV, that the 'counter culture' entered our house. Watts, who had published his first book at nineteen, also wrote about Jung. One Sunday night in the mid-60s, John Freeman's interviews with Carl Jung were broadcast on television. My mother, with, for her, unusual passion, said, 'That man has had a good existence. His life has been fascinating and worthwhile.' For a while Jung's frailties and religious speculations seemed to me to be more interesting than Freud's austerity and sexual speculations.

It was after reading about Jung's experiments with 'word association' that I became interested in 'automatic writing'. When that didn't take me very far, I turned to free assocation as a way of loosening my imagination. Previously, as a writer, I'd laboured under a 'school model', thinking that the harder you pushed to produce significant words and images, the better they'd be.

For my father, during this period, illness meant that there would be the doctor's hurried arrival in the night, his pyjamas protruding from the arms and legs of his suit, followed by the flashing blue light of the ambulance, and the wretched, suddenly diminutive bundle – dad – being laid in the back. I was a teenager, obsessed with my clothes and hair, wondering what I could be for a woman. (In 1974 I wrote in my diary, 'Joanna talking about the day when I went to her house for dinner and said she regretted the fact that I had passed out and gone to sleep, drunk, because she wanted to get to know me more.') With these preoccupations, I could never be sympathetic enough to dad. It is as if your robustness, vigorous curiosity and sexual enthusiasm is an insult to the parent's suffering, to their loss of power and potency. How can you live your life when your father is failing to live his?

But bed is as good a place as any to write. I think my father wrote 'An Indian Adolescence' lying down, with an old children's blackboard propped up in front of him, writing paper clipped to it. When he felt better he'd type it up and carry the work to the post office; then we'd wait. For a while there'd be hope: soon he'd be a successful writer.

The book was discovered by my agent a few months ago. I have no idea how long it had been in her office, but father died nearly eleven years ago. I have not looked at it before. After the age of about sixteen, I didn't read any of his novels and didn't offer him my work to look at. His tough, somewhat sneering criticism was unbearable, and I found myself being too hard on him, too. I would see him getting hurt.

Apart from this, there are kinds of knowing you are cautious of, information about your parents that you're not sure you want to digest, as though all you want to do is make up your mind about them in order to get on with your life. On the other hand, wilful ignorance is no good. I decide that I will see what is in this book. It will be a good way of not rereading Chekhov for a while. My father wouldn't have approved, though. He was hard-working, with powerful wishes, and always made it clear, as did my mother, that they both spent their day doing things they didn't much want to do. Time, therefore, wasn't to be wasted. (Suddenly I recall an odd line in a letter Chekhov wrote to Maxim Gorky: 'You are a young, vigorous, hardy individual; in your place I would be off to India.')

Having studied my parents at close quarters until I was in my late teens, and having thought and dreamt about them most days ever since, a good deal of what I 'know' must be supposition and fantasy. I guess that that is all it ever could be. Therefore, this free-form work of mine is probably closer to fiction than I would like to think. But this research, I hope, will take me much further.

At last I remove the loose typed sheets from the folder, lie down on the sofa in my study, placing a cup of tea where I can reach it, and skim-read the whole book, quickly. Most of it passes without me taking in much detail. But I learn that it is about my father, his parents, and at least one brother. It is set in Poona and Bombay, towards the end of British colonialism. We are 'off to India'.

I walk around the room excitedly. Finding this book is like discovering a trove of forgotten photographs which have to be inspected one by one, in detail. However, people in photographs are silent, and the context and feeling can only be guessed at. In an essay 'Something Given', collected in *Dreaming and Scheming*, I began to write about my father, outside of fiction, for the first time, trying to think about how he wanted to be heard as a writer, and what it meant for our family. But I didn't have objective access to the past like this. I imagine that there is, here – as I seem to be opening a door on the past, preserved in words – some clue or key to my father's life, to the way he lived with my mother, to the nature of my upbringing, and to a political context and colonial relationship. Dad is speaking to me again, and not only from inside my head.

It takes me a day to read it properly. When I do get through it, I am shocked by how much it seems to tell me, and by how much I will have to struggle with now I have stepped into this labyrinth. Will I be different when I come out? More importantly, will dad be different?

CHAPTER TWO

Chapter One of 'An Indian Adolescence' is entitled 'Past Recaptured. End of Thirties'.

There is something I should confront. Although dad's book is written in the third person, switching occasionally, by 'mistake', into the first, I have to say it seems inevitable that I will read his stories as personal truths, if not in the detail then in the feeling. It annoys me, as it might any novelist, to have my own work reduced to autobiography, as though you've just written down what happened. Often, writing isn't always a reflection of experience so much as a substitute for it, an 'instead of' rather than a 'reliving', a kind of daydreaming. The relation between a life and the telling of it is impossible to unravel. Still, whatever my father has made, I will be reconstructing him from these fragments or traces, attempting to locate his 'self' in these imaginings or scatterings. But where else could you look? In Henry James's *Portrait of a Lady* Madame Merle says, 'There's no such thing as an isolated man or woman; we're each of us made up of some cluster of appurtenances. What shall we call our "self"? Where does it begin? Where does it end? It overflows into everything that belongs to us – and then it flows back again.'

I can recall my father insisting, both to me and my agent, that his book was a novel. When my agent suggested that he might increase his chances of having it published if he said it was a

My father as a child

memoir, father continued to argue that it was fiction. 'I am sticking to my guns over this,' he said firmly.

Certainly, the book is full of dialogue, character and dramatised incident. Perhaps father needed it to be a novel because it contained so much truth. In order to speak, he required the disguise of character and imposed narrative. Yet a book, like any work of art, is a series of illusions, and however convinced you are by them, however much you see yourself in the characters and their dilemmas, there is another character behind all the others. This is the concealed author who is everywhere and nowhere, the dreamer himself, the trickster who played the trick, with whom you also identify. As a young man, if I discovered a writer I liked, I'd look out for anything written about him. He or she, as well as the work, then became the subject, the source of the words. If he liked hats, I would think about getting a hat; reading about Scott Fitzgerald always inspired me to go to the pub. The fact is, the place writers and artists hold in the public imagination exists beyond their work.

Whatever sort of book dad has written, there is no denying the trickster's fingerprints are all over it, or that he has done an elemental but traditional thing in trying a self-portrait, an attempt to say something about his life by way of a story with himself at the centre. It is also an invitation to have others see him. But what exactly will I see? People always say more than they mean to. Their words gain their own life, a sort of independent momentum. It is this 'overflowing' I am compelled by.

Eighty pages are missing in the middle. At lunch I ask my mother whether she has a copy. She doesn't. It'll be impossible, I guess, to find them. It is not only those pages which create the effect of an incomplete narrative. If I were my father's editor – which I am now, of course, the two of us working together again as we did in the suburbs, me typing upstairs, him downstairs – I'd say that the material isn't always coherently organised. Father seems to digress and then digress again, failing to return to his starting point as the stories fold in on one another, believing that the reader will want to follow him. 'An Indian Adolescence' has the virtue of reproducing the pattern of his mind rather than the template of other, more orthodox books. It just about holds together enough to be readable, and enjoyable. Father is immersing me in the India of his childhood – and my childhood also, through the stories he told of the India he brought with him.

I think I am writing this book in the way he wrote his, as a sort of collage, hoping the thing holds together, divided and split though it may be, like any mind. Many of the young writers I teach worry about the structure of their work, but I tell them that at the beginning the form of a piece is almost always the least interesting thing about it.

'An Indian Adolescence' begins with a kind of loss. Sixteen-year-old Shani – my father's nickname was Shannoo – is alone in the house in Poona with his mother, while removal men pack up the family belongings. The father, Colonel Murad, has recently resigned as an Army doctor and is now intending to go into business. He has bought a soap factory. Today he is away in Bombay with his other son, Mahmood, where they are organising the new accommodation.

Shani walks through the house and into the garden, wondering what will happen to them all. 'As he walked, he touched the trees – tamarind, mango, neem, peepul and the spreading Banyan. Under them he had studied, chatted, joked and ate raw mangoes with his friends, and was sad that he was leaving them.'

He and his mother, Bibi, are having a religious dispute. Shani's dog has died; Shani has prayed but the dog has not returned. Bibi tells him that if he doesn't believe in prayer he will burn in hell. He seems to know that in challenging his mother's religion he has already rebelled in some important way.

Walking back to his mother, 'he passed through the dining room, drawing room, library. He saw the mahogany tables, chandeliers, leather sofas, Mughal paintings, Chinese vases, Japanese dolls, books, German wine glasses, had all gone.'

I know it must have been unusual for the Kureishi family house to be empty like this. Although there is only one sibling in 'An Indian Adolescence' there were, in fact, twelve children, of which one had died. My father was three or four from the end. Some of the older children had left, but there was plenty of coming and going: to China, England, America and other parts of India. Perhaps father cleared out the rest of the family in order to concentrate on one particular brother, on one representative tension, and that is why he called it a novel.

In Poona – Shannoo at left

Pleased by my discovery of 'An Indian Adolescence', I will show the manuscript to my two elder sons (twins, aged eight) and tell them a bit about it, after school.

If I like to think I live an ordinary bourgeois existence, it doesn't follow that I live in an entirely dull world, which is what I believed about our family life in the London suburbs. In 'An Indian Adolescence' my father and the family are about to leave for the city, Bombay, but I live in London, the city I always yearned to be part of. There is plenty to claim my attention, even when I walk to the shops in the neighbourhood where I have lived for two years – most of which was built for the prosperous middle-class, with their large families and servants, in the mid-Victorian boom.

Wealthy families with au pairs and cleaners own some houses, but many are still divided into flats. Next door lives a Spanish madman who suspends his washing out of the window on a piece of a string. He causes a row when he wrings out his wet underpants over the head of a builder working below.

Some of the houses are 'dole' hotels, packed with Somalian and Eastern European refugees, who sometimes knock at the door, asking for money. There are Lebanese, Japanese, Indian and Chinese restaurants, as well as new fashionable delis and bars. The hairdressers are Portuguese; when my three sons walk past in Brazilian football shirts the owners give us the thumbs-up. The second-hand furniture shops, of which there were many, have turned into twee places selling bags decorated with beads, or 'thank you' cards, where you have to ring a bell to enter. One of the many Asian cornershops has many bare shelves – though there is a good stock of booze in the back – the family sitting in deck chairs out front in the summer; in winter, they light a stinky paraffin heater. As there are several hostels for homeless people in the area, alcoholics and itinerants gather outside this shop early on Sunday mornings, waiting to buy alcohol. Feckless kids linger in the small park, even when it's cold: drinking, fighting, singing; others ride up and down the street on bicycles, trying the handles of the car doors, or smashing car windows.

There are now, as there are everywhere in London, smart bars; but it is the old pubs which show the football. When I go to watch one of Manchester United's European games, before the end of the match, a fight breaks out. The men start to hit each other over the head with stools; several others throw their beer glasses at the wall. As if they do this all the time, the rest of us continue to watch the football, concentrating even more.

In the school playground there are many women wearing the complete hijab, with only slits at the eyes. 'Crows', the children call them. (After the attack on the World Trade Center, some of the Muslim kids would chant Bin Laden's name in the playground.) Other regulars at the playground are a sunken-eyed junkie couple, and a shaven-headed, tattooed man who ties up his dogs outside. There's a writer, a theatre producer, a Rasta, a journalist, and a couple of Czech au pairs with their hair dyed either green or red. When, the other day, one of my sons asked me why they had to go to school, I could only reply: for the social life.

The different communities of London acknowledge and mostly tolerate one another; but except when it's compulsory, in state schools, say, they don't much mix. Perhaps they don't know how to, or can't see the benefit. Still, strolling about London I am amazed by how peaceful and friendly it is, how well the numerous individuals and communities get along without attacking one another. In the face of the difficulties and pressures of everyday life, you'd think there'd be more animosity, more violence. Maybe no one community in this transient part of London feels they have the right to claim exclusive possession over a particular patch of earth, that it's more or less common ground.

Not long ago a friend was telling me how embarrassed she used to be by her father taking her to school, as he stood out so much. At this school, in contemporary London – in Blair's 'inclusive' Britain – it would be impossible to stand out. But, of course, the kids will still be embarrassed by their parents, embarrassed by the love they feel for these awkward creatures, and will not want the other children to see it.

I show the boys my father's manuscript and they talk about being a quarter Indian. They ask me if they're Muslim and put their arms next to mine, to compare colours. They like to declare their Indianness to the other children at school, most of

The twins – Carlo and Sachin – and Kier,
the author's sons

whom are from 'elsewhere'. For my sons – one of whom wears
a baseball cap the wrong way round, does hip-hop poses in the
mirror and makes up 'raps' as he walks home from school – it's
a way of being 'in' with the kids of colour, as well as with the
whites, though these days there isn't much credit in being
English. My children are also beginning to learn that they have
entered a family story, and are curious to see where, and how,
they fit into it.

The second chapter of my father's book is set in Bombay, where
the family has moved. At six in the morning, before leaving for
school, Shani rushes past his brother Mahmood's bedroom and
down to the beach, where he jogs and swims joyfully, before it
gets too hot. There is a Camus-like pleasure in the body and its
relation to the sea, to nature.

Nevertheless, drying himself, he can't help recalling the auc-
tioning of the family possessions. His father, with Bibi watching
from the back of the auction room, holding a yellow parasol,
seemed to have been reduced by it. Shani calls his father 'a non-
entity in his white bush shirt, loose baggy trousers and open

sandals. Out of his uniform he lacked authority, power and arrogance.'

Shani is considering the diminishment of his father when a girl in a blue convent-school uniform passes him, accompanied by her mother. The girl stops and throws a sea shell in the air. She is 'more beautiful than Rita Hayworth and Hedy Lamarr put together'. My father gets an erection, informing him that he seems to have fallen in love. Back at the new house, my father's servant, a randy Leporello-like figure in a voluminous gallabiya and greasy fez, tells Shani that he knows the girl's maid. The family has only recently moved nearby. My father is pleased; he might be able to see her again. The girl is called Muni.

The book's increasingly sexual tone continues with a strange episode. It is set during Holi, a Hindu festival, and involves Shani, his best friend Masood – he sounds like Mahmood, I know, but he is not – and 'the newly refurbished Peacock restaurant'. This café is their regular haunt, where dad and his pals go to gossip. The owner, an Iranian known as Irani, fancies Masood and tries to seduce him. Irani is 'dressed in a black short shirt with pink flowers, purple satin trousers, a shrill green scarf tied round his neck, and a scout on a string over it. His hairy ears were stuffed with bits of cotton wool, soaked in some sweet atar, a kind of oily Iranian perfume.'

Masood goes up to Irani's room. My father isn't there, but nonetheless describes the filthy place in some detail, with its smell of the local hooch, made from date palm, and 'a picture of some god surrounded in light hung on the wall'. Masood puts a sleeping potion into Irani's drink. As Irani begins to pass out, Masood ties a pink balloon around Irani's penis,

23

leads him downstairs, shoves him naked into the restaurant, and flees.

Like almost all the stories in that great collection of Muslim tales, the *Arabian Nights*, dad's little story concerns desire and the humiliation which follows it. As in one of my favourite films, Buñuel's *That Obscure Object of Desire*, it shows that to act at all, to be lured, enticed by desire in the shape of another, is to will not only failure and dissatisfaction, but punishment. This is always comic – in others. I wonder if this droll anecdote, oddly placed in the narrative, is some sort of motif. I look forward to more of it, and can imagine dad laughing as he described the incident, pulling up his shirt and slapping his fat stomach.

Behind this comedy, of course, and often forgotten, is the omniscient cynical author, who is well aware of this cycle of demand and degradation and can only recount these stories, not to illuminate human foolishness, which is almost impossible, but because there is nothing better to do.

Meanwhile Shani is on his way to school. In Poona dad and his brother Omar had attended a Catholic missionary school where they were taught by Jesuits. They were driven to school in a horse-drawn carriage with a groom to carry their cricket, polo and boxing kit. Now, walking in their new city of Bombay, a 'short cut' takes Shani through a colony of shacks built of corrugated sheets, cardboard boxes and old crates. He picks his way over 'the sick, the poor, the crippled and the homeless' who sleep there. Shani says he ignores them, as does everyone, but clearly it disturbs him. His 'privileged, comfort-able' life makes him feel guilty. He is relieved to see 'the small, white Apollo cinema with a zinc roof, where they were showing *How Green Was My Valley* – by popular request'. At the end of the film, of course, it was compulsory to stand for the British national anthem.

Shani takes the train into Churchgate, in the centre of Bombay, but has to travel second-class. In the London suburbs my father was a commuter for thirty years. After a ten-minute walk past the hedges and garages of the suburban houses – each of which seemed to disgorge, every morning, a man in a bowler hat and raincoat, carrying an umbrella – dad had to take a bus to the station. The journey from our local station, Bromley South, to Victoria took about twenty minutes, depending on whether you caught a fast or slow train. The whole trip to work took more than an hour each way. Dad used the time to read; sometimes he would talk bitterly of what it was like standing in the crowded second-class carriage, a sick old man, when there were seats available in first. These twice-a day train trips, and the preparation and recuperation they required, set the grid for our daily life. I had no idea that he had already experienced these daily journeys in India.

Now, squeezed between 'shop assistants with tiffin-carriers resting on their laps, the corridors blocked by beggars, urchins and young boys', he recalls a three-day train trip he took with his father and brother Mahmood, to Delhi. On that occasion his father was in full uniform:

His brass crown and stars shone on the shoulders of his khaki jacket. His khaki shirt, starched stiff as a poker, had red patches on the collar, a khaki tie and a shining Sam Browne belt round his slim waist. A Malacca stick was in his hand. A batman, to cater for his needs on the train, carried his trench coat, brief case and a small attaché case.

At nine in the evening the batman came in with whisky and

soda, bottles of beer, lemonade, thick beef and hard-boiled egg sandwiches, white folded napkins on a big tray.

On the Churchgate train, which was already jammed, British soldiers, 'anxious lest some Indian nationalist tossed a bomb on the train', would occasionally join the commuters. Recently, among the British soldiers, there was an almost black Indian soldier whom Shani's friend Masood called an Uncle Tom. When the British soldiers referred to this man as 'Eric', Shani and Masood realised he was an Indian Christian, a convert from the Untouchable class. Masood had told him he should be emptying 'shit pots'.

The theme of class, or ambiguity as to one's social status – questions about when one can identify with a group – continues as Shani finally arrives at 'Broadfields', the English public school he attends, run by British teachers. The history teacher, called Ted Pritchard, is a cockney from Walthamstow, and the Indian boys are fond of him. Dad says, 'Poor Pritchard was never made to forget he was working class, even though he was fourteen thousand miles away from England. Shani had once heard another teacher say, "I wish old Ted wouldn't roll his cigarettes in public. It gives the natives the wrong impression of us."'

Britain is such a melange of accents now, it would be hard to imagine such attitudes, partly because people's accents change so rapidly. When my sons return from school they can sound Jamaican. 'Hush your mouth there, bwoy,' they say. At other times they sound like Little Lord Fauntleroy. I was alarmed when I overheard one of their au pairs imitating their middle-class accents. Perhaps race, rather than class, is where we have currently decided to argue about what differences mean.

The chapter ends with Shani, who we learn is school cricket captain, being begged by a boy called Visram, the son of a powerful and influential man, to be included in the cricket team. When my father refuses – the kid can't play well – Visram's mother visits the family house in order to have it out with my very religious grandmother, Bibi – a woman I never met. I want to know more about her.

CHAPTER THREE

A few days after I began on this exploration – I don't know what else to call it – something serendipitous occurred which opens another door.

Of the twelve Kureishi children – most of whom lived in the house in Poona – four are alive: the two sisters, and my uncles Omar and Tootoo. Tootoo, who now lives in Canada, emails me to say that Omar, living in a small flat in Karachi, has written two volumes of autobiography, *Once upon a Time* and *As Time Goes By*. They are published, so far, only in Pakistan. Apparently they are 'bestsellers'.

I ring Omar, whom I have not seen since the mid-1980s. His voice, once one of the most famous in India, now sounds reedy and thin. But he declares himself happy to be alive and working, wonders how much longer he has to live, and sends his books to me. When they arrive, I notice that *Once upon a Time* covers the period my father is writing about. On the jacket is an Indian boy of about nine, a beach, Bombay's Gateway to India and the British, Indian and Pakistani flags. The jacket of the second volume includes reviews of the first, one of which says, 'One salutes Omar Kureishi for telling his story exceptionally well and without any apologies. The oracle has spoken.'

There is, of course, a long and fascinating history of middle-class Indians writing about what V. S. Naipaul calls 'the enigma of arrival' – their lives as Indians in Britain and America, the stranger's view from underneath. There is that; but there is much more. It occurs to me that Omar might be 'Mahmood' in my father's novel, and I begin to wonder what it is he wants to say about this brother.

Roger Michell, who directed *The Buddha of Suburbia* for the BBC, is now preparing a film I've written, *The Mother*. Although I sat with him as he cast the film, he doesn't much like writers being on set. Different directors have different views on this. However, my twin sons are playing one part, a character called Jack, and I go to visit whichever one is working that day, at lunchtime. They must have watched a movie a day for years now, and I'm happy for them to learn how films are made. It amuses me that they find it hard to combine the lethargy and inactivity of waiting with the sudden demand for a performance.

Part of *The Mother*'s story concerns a mother and daughter who disagree about their shared past. The daughter has been in therapy and has come to resent the mother for neglecting her as a child. What interested me is the wild divergence of people's accounts of the past, so much so that these seem like quite different stories.

My two eldest sons, identical twins who have more or less the same experience, will give uncannily similar answers to the same question, using the same words. But their answers will also be different, with, usually, different demands at the end of them. With such thoughts in my head, and full of curiosity, I begin to read Omar's book alongside my father's.

Some sort of search is beginning. I guess you don't really go looking for your parents until middle age. For me, this has become a quest, for my place in father's history and fantasy, and for the reasons my father lived the semi-broken life he did. I'm looking for the way in which a particular adult life is a response to childhood, an answer to the questions that this particular childhood asked. From this point of view an adult is someone who had an overwhelming childhood, and renewal means remembering, filling in the gaps, in order to forget for good.

'I write for a living,' Omar used to say. 'That's all there is to it. End of story.'

As an adolescent, I was enraptured by a black-and-white photograph of my most glamorous uncle Omar on the cover of a collection of his essays, *Out to Lunch*. Wearing an open-necked shirt and smoking, Omar was sitting at a portable typewriter, a glass of whisky beside him. It was, I guess, a Hemingwayesque pose. It was the mid to late 1960s; there were wars which writers went to; writers were public figures, the exemplars being Baldwin, Mailer, Malraux, Vidal, Sartre.

In the suburbs conversation was not encouraged. There was a lot that shouldn't be said. It was the women who talked. But when dad took me to London to visit Omar, the other brothers and their friends, the conversation, aided by alcohol, was lively and loud, and conducted in three languages, Urdu, English and Urdu-English. It was so full of jokes, witticisms, filthy stories and political comment about both Britain and Pakistan, and gossip about sport – a extemporary surreal flow – that I saw that conversation was not the exchange of information, but a masculine pleasure, an exercise in imagination and knowledge even. The men sat down to do it, for hours, and it was thrilling. Speaking didn't come naturally to anyone; you had to learn to be good at it. I can recall one of my uncles saying to me, 'Why can't you entertain us like this?'

Omar

At almost eighty, Omar is still a working journalist, and his columns are syndicated all over South-East Asia. India and Pakistan have remained predominantly print cultures longer than the West. The main source of information and political argument has been newspapers rather than the heavily censored television, though this is changing.

I have decided to put my father's novel aside in order to read Omar's memoir, wondering how the two brothers' accounts will compare and whether they cover the same territory. Immediately I see that my uncle's approach is different to my father's. Omar begins by saying that the British Raj – 'founded on the certainty of a racial and moral superiority over the natives' – will be the central character of his account of pre-Partition India. His book will be concerned with a political link, and with what power does to those who have it and to those who don't. According to Omar, the British, ordinary enough in their own country, change as they pass through the Suez Canal. 'Eastwards of Port Said they became empire-builders.' In other words, leaving home enabled them to become different, more powerful, people. Enoch Powell, who arrived in Delhi a bit later, in 1943, understood the lure of these enlarging transformations when he wrote in a letter, 'I shall leave India with real reluctance, partly because every Englishman in India has ipso facto a certain value, but mainly because of the unending fascination of this incredible Empire in which potentially we have in our hands power and wealth that would make America seem insignificant, and where nevertheless an evil spell seems to bind both the land itself and us.'

Omar's autobiography is a benign view; his 'writing voice' is temperate, witty and informative. Nevertheless, his book contains no other voices, either other parts of himself or other speaking characters, which would be the case in a novel. As my father seemed to be insisting, the novel, being a conflictual form, is a natural outlet for drama, for internal dispute and multiple viewpoints.

It isn't long before my grandfather – Colonel Murad in dad's rendition – enters Omar's record. Educated at King's College, London (where I went, though dad never told me his father had been there), Omar says of him, 'My father was an Army Colonel who belonged to the elite Indian Medical Service and this made him something of a sahib, though more properly he was a member of an emerging middle class of professionals as opposed to the comic aristocracy of the ruling princes and the landed gentry. He believed in the family as a unit; there was no sibling rivalry.'

During the First World War my grandfather was based in Tientsin, northern China, where three of the boys were born. Eventually the family was posted back to India. My father was born in Madras, before the family moved to Poona. As I read, I am surprised to find my father turning up almost immediately. He has a gun pointing at him, having provoked a British tommie at a cricket match.

In Poona most of the family had been together, which is perhaps why father finds the empty house, at the beginning of his own account, so disturbing. I learn from Omar that it was in Poona that the family started their own cricket team, Colonel Kureishi's XI, with other Hindu, Parsi, Christian and Jewish boys joining them occasionally. For Omar, cricket is political; it is where the British can be beaten at their own game. According to my father, Mahmood/Omar often brings home 'progressive

Colonel Kureishi with the author's mother

Marxists who'd smoke State Express 555, drink gin, and discuss poverty, equality and the Bengal Famine'. This radicalism, mocked by dad, also alarms their mother Bibi, who fears it will turn them against Islam.

In Omar's book Colonel Kureishi's XI play against British Army units, the Reformatory School and the Mental Hospital ('the staff, not the inmates'). Team discussions are held in the Irani restaurant.

In 1987 I took a steam train, the Deccan Queen, from Bombay to Poona. The next day I found what I wanted to believe had been the family house, a huge place, with a long drive and a lot of land, servants squatting in the shade. A few doors down, to my surprise, I came to the commune of the Bhagwan Shree Rajneesh, whose books my father was enthusiastic about. If Western priests and philosophers would not, or could not, speak about how to live, the curious could go to Indian gurus. I asked to be shown around, and a serious and silent guard with a whistle around his neck accompanied me everywhere, refusing to answer questions.

Although Rajneesh, along with his jewel-encrusted cap and vast collection of Rolls-Royces, had decamped to the US in 1980 – he was arrested and expelled in 1985 – I'd noticed dozens of orange-robed youngsters walking around Poona. Like a lot of people, I'd become interested in Tantra, the idea that all energy is libido. Rajneesh was well known for pioneering the idea of 'spiritual sexuality', which had led to stories of partner exchange, group sex and general weirdness. His cult may have had its origins in the 1960s, but in typical 1980s style Rajneesh had turned himself into a celebrity and was selling himself via

34

merchandise: tapes, books and videos. Some of these tapes I played to the actor Roshen Seth in the early 1990s, when we were rehearsing the film version of *The Buddha of Suburbia*. He incorporated something of Rajneesh's strangely quiet, almost hissing tone into the character of the father. However, amongst Rajneesh's people paranoia had set in, and the Poona commune resembled a strictly run American campus, with glowering guards and the tone of a party which had long ended.

In India, I had powerful, disturbing dreams of my father's death. Next morning I couldn't get out of bed: I felt as though my spine had been twisted by a giant. The doctor gave me pain killers and, later, I visited a yogi with hypnotic eyes, who chanted and hummed cheerily, telling me to imagine a rose with dew on it, a golden egg in the flame of a candle and a lotus blossom in red.

I notice from my diary that I had, at this point, begun what I called my 'Buddha book', of which I'd completed around 12,000 words. Although I had wanted to follow my father in his philosophical speculations, I had a mind less susceptible to such ideas, preferring to take a comic view of dad and of the flourishing 'New Age' which appeared to be replacing both traditional religion and the 60s counter-culture among the young.

I must return now to 'An Indian Adolescence'. My grandmother is about to be confronted by Visram's mother, who has visited in order to criticise my father for excluding her son from the cricket team. Father writes, 'A few minutes later, Bibi came down into the drawing room. Her head was covered in a green dupata and she wore a clean, freshly ironed kurta and kameez. She had her prayer beads in her hand.'

Bibi defends my father's right to pick whoever he likes for the team he captains. Visram's pushy mother is dismissed, and peremptorily too, and dad feels vindicated. Then Bibi, my father and Mahmood/Omar walk along the beach to visit the family of the Convent girl – Muni – who my father saw throwing and catching sea shells. Dad has dressed suitably for the occasion in his 'nigger brown corduroy trousers, cream coloured silk shirt, a faint green silk scarf round his neck, light brown socks and his two-tone white-and-tan shoes, with thick rubbery soles'. He thinks he's the cat's whiskers. His brother Omar/Mahmood, as any brother might, calls him 'a pimp on the make'.

Shockingly, at the house, seeing the ravishing Muni again – 'her plaits rested on her shoulders and she wore a bright red rose in her hair, close to her ear' – my father instantly has a dev-astating attack of self-doubt. He has 'no great looks, personal-ity, charm, sex appeal or even any kind of talent'. He is not only gloomy, while Mahmood confidently discusses Pearl Buck and Somerset Maugham with Muni, but seems to have lost his soul.

Omar stated 'there was no sibling rivalry'. But how could there not be? What is he afraid of seeing here? There are always two brothers – Romulus and Remus, Cain and Abel – and one of them murders the other. At least I am being made aware of the division of labour between them. In my father's account Mahmood/Omar will have the good qualities, 'charm, good looks, intelligence and personality'. Shani thinks of how Mahmood is the son adored by the parents; he is excellent at sports, his studies and the tango; he can even jive, and adores Fats Waller. He speaks of himself as a future Foreign Secretary of Free India. Dad's gloom doesn't lift; how could it? When

Shani, mocking his brother, pretends to throw up, Mahmood glares at Shani, a look which reminds Shani of his father: 'You shivered and sometimes wet your pants.'

At last Shani interrupts his own thoughts by asking Muni's brother about an orange badge on his shirt, bearing the initials RSS. The brother says this stands for 'Rashtiya Swayamsevah Sangh'. The family are part of a Hindu Revival Movement.

The brother explains: 'We believe that India is for the Hindus. That's why it is known as Hindustan. We're therefore against Pakistan. We will fight that opportunist Jinnah. He's a British Agent, paid to create trouble and delay Independence. We will destroy the Muslim League and its stooges. That's why we're training hard.'

Bibi replies pluckily, 'Listen, you little Hindu Bania. We are not going to allow the likes of you to absorb us. You have your Hindustan. We have our Pakistan. And don't you ever say anything against the Muslims in my presence, you hear?'

My father, disturbed by these divisions within the Indians, and having envisaged, after the exorcism of Powell's 'evil spell', a 'Free India, democratic, fair and equal', also comments, 'Let's see what Sir Stafford Cripps brings.'

A little later Bibi leaves, but the party continues. Shani does finally speak to Muni and discovers that she is a socialist, influenced by Shaw's *An Intelligent Woman's Guide to Socialism*. She declares, 'Freedom of India also means freedom for Indian women.' Clearly, British feminism and socialism were influencing the Indian middle class: at around the same time, in England, Jawaharlal Nehru and his daughter Indira were visiting the British Fabians, represented by Shaw's friends and colleagues, the Webbs. Nehru writes: 'It was almost a pilgrimage, for the Webbs occupy a unique place not only in England but in the world of international socialism.'

The next morning, after swimming and running, Shani declares that the disorder of love has been too much for him. He's only met Muni twice and all he feels is envy, loss and longing. 'This new kind of aggressive Indian woman wasn't for him. They frightened him.' Just then, however, he bumps into her on the beach, accompanied by her Goanese maid. Muni is as serious as before and tells him that he should commit himself to 'India's struggle'. She goes on, 'The trouble with you, Shani, is that you go to an English public school. The slavish imitation of the English is the curse of the Indian upper classes.'

Then she tells him to remind Mahmood to bring round the book he promised to lend her.

I sit in the park watching my three sons play football, and find myself admiring the pleasures they have. I think of the three of them together as adults, with their children, sharing this history, always having one another. As a boy with one sister and a mother who is an only child, I was fascinated by dad's large family, by the cricket teams, the swimming, the companionship of the brothers. A number of my close male friendships have been attempts to recreate what I imagined was a 'brotherhood'.

My father, having lived the reality, doesn't share my fantasies. I can't help but find it disturbing, this powerful and furious envy of his brother. Dad seems to be very competitive, but there's something about competing that he can't bear. Later, although he continues to see his brothers, he retreats to the London suburbs. Perhaps father wanted to begin a new life, discontinuous with the old, without religion or the past, without his own language, like those people in films who attempt to make a new identity by pretending to be someone else – usually someone they've murdered. But it doesn't work: at the end of his life he writes this 'novel' in which his competitiveness, and the feeling of failure which accompanies it, seems to be as fresh and potent as ever.

I wonder whether this is 'the wound' he seemed to be nursing when I was a child, the feeling of defeat and inferiority he tried to overcome by becoming a writer, and by having me become one. Omar, in his account, doesn't recall any of this going on, but then it isn't his intention to give us the low-down on the family conflicts. For him, emotional strife is focused around colonialism and cricket. It is the British, not the father or the brothers, who have the power he wants to escape. It is into 'the British' that he puts the bad things.

I am, however, startled by father's feeling of failure so early on. Certainly, he is good at cricket, as his brother and 'rival' explains. The next time dad turns up in Omar's *Once upon a Time*, he is playing in an important cricket match against the Bombay Gymkhana. According to Ramachanra Guha in his book *A Corner of a Foreign Field*, the Gymkhana was formed in 1875, consolidating 'into a single institution, separate polo, cricket, football and rifle clubs run for and by whites'. In 1877 the scene was described in the *Bombay Gazette*:

Hundreds of natives, chiefly Parsees, were gathered beneath the trees that skirt the cricket ground – surely with its brilliant verdure and splendid surrounding buildings one of the liveliest in the world – and in the Gymkhana tents there was a numerous company of Europeans. In the afternoon the ground bore a singularly lively appearance. Thousands of natives took up a position wherever they could get a glimpse of the players, and

39

whenever a hit or a catch was made, they yelled with an enthusiasm that bespoke much for the future of cricket among them in Bombay.

There seems little doubt that my father was a better cricketer than Omar, a fact for which Omar gives my father credit, though dad didn't seem able to accept it. Omar writes, 'Bombay Gymkhana was a "For Europeans Only" club. It was a great honour for us Indians to be allowed in its hallowed premises. The star of the team was my brother Shannoo. In one match he took eight wickets and the *Evening News* did a feature on him with the headline "School Boy Who Bowls Googlies". He had bowled a batsman with a googly and when the batsman was asked what happened he said the ground shook.'

I want to think about this and, as my father does, digress a little.

My parents met in 1952. Mother was living with her parents in the suburbs while working as a painter for a local potter. Dad had already started at the Embassy, in Knightsbridge, and was living in a bedsit in Wood Green, North London. He was friendly with a Pakistani naval officer who was engaged to a friend of mother's, an art teacher. The four of them would go out together, eating and dancing at Maxim's, near Victoria Station. I know dad played cricket when he first came to England, after Partition. I can remember photographs of him holding his bat up, being applauded on some local cricket ground. But I don't think my mother liked either sitting in damp pavilions, or being a 'cricket widow'. She was never afraid to stand up for herself; she had, after all, married an Indian for which, presumably, she had received some disapproval, though full-blown racism didn't begin until later. However, mother's family wasn't sporty: my

Author's father and mother, 1953

maternal grandfather had owned antiques and grocery shops, and my maternal grandmother worked in the local post office all her life; she had also been in the Salvation Army. I have no memory of dad playing cricket competitively. But mother was taken, when pregnant with me, to at least one match. The

Pakistani opener, Hanif Mohammed, known by his friends as Dilip, after the Bombay film star Dilip Kumar, was playing. She liked the name Hanif.

So, in England, my father began his own family or empire. At home he could be the father he wished he'd had – involved, attentive, guiding – rather than the remote figure he describes Colonel Murad as being. Colonel Kureishi gambled every day and talked of becoming a professional poker player. He played cards with Omar; Omar knew it was the one thing that cheered him up. But my father hated card games and said it was self-destructive, the gambler wanted to lose. Dad didn't like me playing card games either. Risk wasn't dad's thing. In Bromley he seemed to be living his life in the negative, as though there was someone bad inside him. Moreover, he was more isolated than he'd ever been before, and, somehow, this played itself out through me.

In the late 50s and early 60s, in our little garden in the sub-urbs, my father spent a lot of time coaching me at cricket, teaching me the shots, showing me how to hold the bat and ball, and throwing balls so I could practise catching and fielding. In my kitchen I can still 'do' a googly, and even a Chinaman (a left-handed googly). More than this, I remember arguments and the terrible humiliation he made me feel. I'd have hysterical crying fits, little breakdowns, tantrums. Tennis racquets and cricket bats would get smashed. When, later, I saw Pete Townshend destroying his guitar on stage, or heard Hendrix playing 'The Star Spangled Banner' at Woodstock, I felt I knew exactly what was going on. I came to like disruptive moments in a work of art, when the discourse broke down and the stories exploded into chaos.

Author's father in cricketing gear, with
unknown Englishman

My father was, essentially, a teacher, captivated by how one learned. But the position of teacher is never unambiguous. At the very least one person has the power and the other doesn't; the teacher has something the pupil either does or does not want. Reading father's book I am becoming aware that, partly, I was being made to feel as he had felt. He might want me to be successful, as his father had required him to be, but he was afraid of me becoming too powerful or rivalrous. He didn't, for instance, want me to turn into his brother who was more talented and, moreover, something of a boaster and show-off, a

43

man who could bear being enviable. If I was to be a brother to dad, I had to be the weak, little one, the role he had had thrust on him. At the same time I had to be good company, and educable. Really, I was to be like him in every way; if we deviated, there would be trouble.

And so the cricket I played was alone, in the back garden. Father and I fixed a cricket ball to a piece of string and tied it to the branch of an apple tree. I would hit the ball with a broom handle. Dad told me the Australian genius Bradman had done this, to improve his accuracy.

Obediently, I would do this for hours and hours, after school and at weekends, in all weathers. I'd play games in my head, and would write down the scores of imaginary teams ('Hunte, Sobers, Kanhai, Kureishi . . . .') in a scorebook, while whispering an imaginary radio commentary to myself in Omar's accent and locutions. (He was, by now, working as a cricket commentator for BBC radio.)

Being alone in this way, making things up, might, inadvertently, have prepared me for being a writer, for the solitary pleasures of creativity. None of it prepared me for the pace or spin of a real cricket ball, of which I was afraid, or for the competitiveness of an actual match. On the rare occasions when I did go out to play, at school or in the local park, I was scared, useless and ashamed. I could play some pretty shots, my hands and feet were in the right place, but I wasn't competitive enough. When father asked me how I had done, I never wanted to own up, and my mother had to protect me from my father's mockery and pity. 'Oh, leave him alone,' she'd say.

But father persisted and would take me around cricket clubs in Kent, trying to get me a game, which he did, on occasions.

Far from any bus stop there would be rotting pavilions which smelled of socks; there'd be big West Indian fast bowlers, cucumber sandwiches and milky tea. Dad would stand on the boundary watching, shouting instructions and encouragement, as I, usually freezing cold, struggled not to fail, attempting not to make him disappointed, knowing he could do better than I. I'd also sit with him at the Oval and Lords, watching Test cricket, or at home, with the radio, listening to Omar commentating on the Pakistan matches.

At the same time, confusingly, father would say he didn't envy professional cricketers or any sportsmen for that matter. Their careers ended early, and they had nothing important to do for the rest of their lives – as, perhaps, father's 'career' as a schoolboy cricketer was over and those past glories, the cups and newspaper reports, meant nothing but relative diminishment now. In England, it seemed as though he had to start again, which was both a liberation and a curse. The idea of being a writer replaced the idea of being a cricketer, for me as for him.

I failed at cricket, deliberately I hope. But only I knew how big a failure it was. To everyone else, if I wasn't much good at it, what did it matter? But father had gone to a lot of trouble to initiate me into this game, into this family ideal and passion, and, to do him a favour, I let him down. I see it still as my own foolish failure rather than as a father's unconscious contrivance.

A real insurgent would have rebelled properly. 'What is a rebel?' asks Camus, himself a keen sportsman. 'A man who says no; but whose refusal does not imply a renunciation. He is also a man who says yes as soon as he begins to think for himself.'

Revolt as discontent, as anguish, as individualism not conformity; thinking one's own thoughts as opposed to following others. Writing this book I wonder what my self consists of. I feel inhabited by others, composed of them. Writers, parents, older men, friends, girlfriends, speak inside me. If I took them away, what would be left? I think of the essential work of imitation, differentiation and opposition, and how it never stops. Also, the puzzling thing about rebellion is that the order you wish to defy is so deep and hidden within yourself that you cannot even begin to know it. The only reality it has is of fear and phobia. How, then, to begin to live differently?

It has taken me a long time to formulate my own 'yeses'. Although I have little interest in cricket now, I feel guilty that I don't know which Test team is touring England; I don't even know who the players are, though I often put myself to sleep running through the names of English, Australian and Pakistani teams of the 60s. The last time I went to watch a Test match, sitting on a hard bench in light rain all day, I found it odd to be in a place so full of people who'd brought their own sandwiches, and so few of them women. And, although my sons and I are in the park most weekends, we never play or watch cricket. They don't even know the rules, or why cricket has been an important Indian and family sport. (My son Sachin is, however, named after an Indian cricketer.) Now and again, when I find myself standing with my arms around one of my sons, attempting to show him how to take a cricket stance, I find myself turning away in confusion. I like football, as did dad, though he found it a little 'lower class'.

Anyhow, I was beginning to love the Rolling Stones and, although later I knew that Mick Jagger and the Pakistan captain and all-rounder Imran Khan would sit together in the pavilion at Lords, I could, at the time, use the sexuality and defiance of the Stones and other groups to move away from the conflicts that cricket stirred in me.

These failures stay with you, particularly if you don't know the source of their power. Later, I could join my father's desire, discovering something that pleased both him and myself and which we could collaborate seriously on, Chekhov and writing, for instance.

At the time I was at a newly built suburban secondary modern school which put the emphasis on practical subjects such as woodwork, metalwork and technical drawing. Our class and position in society was made pretty clear from the first day. When not doing 'practical' learning, we were either copying from the blackboard or attempting to follow 'dictation'. We were not even oppressed by the imposition of moral or religious axioms, or even ideas of 'good' behaviour. We were aware that we were existing in a very banal dictatorship; this, in its own way, might be described as educational. Otherwise, we were only filling paper, and filling time. There was nothing to be done with the information we received; it was inert, dead. How could it become part of a living system? Nobody knew, including the teachers, how to ask why we were there or what we should be doing. The only good teacher was the rock star Peter Frampton's father, who taught art. I did learn about all kinds of music from the radio in my bedroom, which was on constantly; there seemed to be a lot of good things on the radio then. It wasn't impossible, therefore, to pick up knowledge, if school hadn't completely discouraged you.

Every day I was afraid to go to school because I knew the

47

authentic life of the school existed beneath the surface, in the constant brutality and bullying of the boys, in their sexuality, in that of the masters, and in the punishments – desire by other means. There were strange, sadistic and almost ritualistically weird beatings, where three or four boys would be bent forward at the front of the class while the maths teacher would stand over them, stick raised, asking the rest of us which bottom should be beaten. The teacher had two 'beaters', of different lengths and thicknesses, called 'big Willy' and 'little Willy'. We knew by the charged, euphoric and unpedagogical atmosphere that this was neither informative nor decent, but it was certainly enlightening. Mother's question, 'What did you do at school today?', was, in a sense, unanswerable. I began to see that silence could be useful; it could be awful, too, like being bricked up, though the consequences of this would take a while to become clear.

I was sent to this school – as a punishment, it seemed to me – because from about the age of seven or eight I found it impossible to learn. I couldn't retain any knowledge; the frustration of waiting and listening made me unbearably confused. I'd become phobic about teachers, partly because they were incapable, like my parents, of protecting me from racial bullying. I was called 'lazy', or it was thought I had something wrong with my eyes. My skin was blotchy and I developed twitches, tics and numerous stomach complaints. Like Shani's mother, my own mother had withdrawn – although she was born only yards from where we lived, and it was she, rather than my father, who first took me to the local libraries, she had been to art school, and had studied art in Paris. But then she lost hope; she wouldn't draw, or engage with others. Nothing would go into either of us for fear, perhaps, it would turn us into people father didn't recognise. 'Being there for him' meant being someone he could play with. I was reading randomly but compulsively, yet for years had the odd feeling of being 'stuck' in some way, as though there was a point beyond which I couldn't go. There were lots of things I couldn't think about – race, sexuality, my parents – things which I couldn't process but which seemed jammed inside me: another kind of silence, feeling without words.

My father found his own satisfaction in books, and in his burgeoning ambition as a writer. Dad never went to Pakistan, not even for a holiday. He never saw his mother again. Rejoining his family would be too difficult. But he was, in the mornings and weekends, writing two books, which were published, about the 'homeland' the rest of his family had moved to. For him, reading and writing about his country were enough. That was the distance he liked; instead of living, he began to write about those who lived.

I say 'never went to Pakistan', but dad had passionately complicated feelings about the place. In the early 1980s, when, at Omar's urging, I decided to go, my father was furious: betrayed, abandoned, humiliated by his envy. I can recall sitting in a room in Karachi, a few weeks later, with five of the brothers. I was wearing, as I can see from photographs taken then, one of my father's suit jackets. My whole time there was spent in a condition of heightened anxiety, so I was delighted when my uncles told me how much I resembled them, and how I fitted in right away. My father's absence burned. Where was he? What was he doing? Why couldn't he get here?

*

I like to think of dad sitting with his back to me in his room in our house, writing at his desk. He turns when I come in, or, concentrating, just says, 'Hi boy, what have you been doing?' He likes to see me; he pulls my nose and squeezes my cheeks; he wants to talk.

Now, in 'An Indian Adolescence', father is in a similar position – at his desk in his room in Bombay, sitting under a photograph of the Australian genius Don Bradman, reading the essays of Charles Lamb. Dad writes, 'Occasionally Shani would look up to see what was happening on the beach. He loved the sight of rain falling on the grey sea, the thin smokey mist and the smell of seaweed in salt.' In *Once upon a Time* Omar calls Juhu almost a private beach, but 'there would be makeshift stalls selling green coconuts. In the monsoons, we could see the dark rain-clouds approaching, as if from behind the horizon.'

Not unlike other Indians of his class, my father liked to read about London, wondering what it would be like to go there. In his *Autobiography*, Gandhi wrote, in 1927, 'Time hung heavily on my hands in Bombay. I dreamt continually of going to England.' In *The Autobiography of An Unknown Indian*, published in 1963, Nirad C. Chaudhuri describes a romantic vision of England as seen from India, a series of names from history books: Shakespeare, Cromwell, Wordsworth, Queen Victoria, Kipling, He also describes an ambivalence. 'The prevalent attitude towards Englishmen of our people was one of irrational and ineradicable cringing and equally irrational and unconquerable hatred. Grown-ups reserved the first for the Englishmen present before them and the second for the absent Englishmen.' He adds – and this would be something the Muslims of India, already thinking about Pakistan, would be aware of – 'The Hindu regards himself as heir to the oldest conscious tradition of superior colour and as the carrier of the purest and most exclusive stream of blood which created that colour, by whose side the Nazi was a mere parvenu.'

Sitting at his desk, Shani ponders what he will do with his life. Mahmood is planning to study for the Bar in London. But Colonel Murad wants my father to attend the Military Academy, which dad isn't keen to do.

Dad looks at himself: 'Perhaps Shani had a talent for something. But if he did have a gift, it lay buried within, suppressed by other people's views, opinions, ideas and influences.' As with his mother, he believes Muni has no interest in him. He becomes even harder on himself:

> At times, his facial expressions gave the impression of timidity, his eyes of fright, his manners tentative, his actions indecisive, his views half-baked, his attitude negative, and they all gave a collective impression of a boy who was weak, indifferent, casual, aimless, going nowhere, and which made his father remark that he was useless.

Just then his servant, humming an Indian film song, bursts into the room and tells Shani that Colonel Murad wants to see him. Dad is terrified, and writes, 'If Shani had learnt anything in the English public school, it was to be cool. Take nothing or anybody seriously. Consider yourself better than the others.' So that's what they teach them in those places. However, Shani can't help thinking, as he washes, combs his hair and changes his clothes, of how his father goes around the house inspecting the rooms, as though still in the army barracks. Colonel Murad often went 'mad':

> His father had only to stare at him for a moment or raise his

voice, and Shani would tremble, turn ashen. It was pure fear. If he said that he wanted to see him in the morning, he couldn't sleep. He would lay awake all night, worrying about it. His body would go numb . . .

Certainly, several of my uncles had 'volcanic' tempers, including Omar. I was mesmerised by these uncontrolled displays of pure demand. I guess they reminded me of my cricket breakdowns, but also of what is lost in suburban restraint. For some reason, my father was proud of his self-control. His violence, like mine, was manifested in sulking, silence and staring at people. But he did practise what he called 'deep-breathing techniques' to keep unwanted furies at bay.

Now, 'Shani entered the drawing room with trepidation. The double doors towards the balcony were opened and he could see the sky had darkened and a few drops of rain began to fall.'

Luckily for Shani, his father is not alone but with Niazi, a cousin who is in the army. 'There were three stars on his shoulder straps, a short three coloured ribbon above his bulging pocket. His peaked cap was on the floor.' Unlike his father and Mahmood, Niazi always cheers Shani up. One time, together, they even shot a snake, which surprises me, as I can't imagine dad shooting anything. But there is, regrettably, no account of it.

Shani listens to Niazi and his father. Niazi had been stationed in Tobruk. It was a hard battle; Rommel was a great general, but he ran out of fuel. Shani knows so well what envy is; he is afraid that Colonel Murad will be depressed by Niazi's exploits. When Colonel Murad brings up an old story about fighting the Afghan tribesmen near the Khyber, Niazi sneaks a look at his watch.

To Shani's pleasure, rather than scolding him, Colonel Murad has called him in to suggest that Shani accompany Niazi on a shopping trip. As soon as the two of them take off in the old black Ford, Niazi says, 'Have you fucked a woman yet?'

'No,' says Shani. 'But I know a few girls.'

Niazi tells him that the world at the moment is a dangerous place. He has heard – we don't know how, but perhaps Mahmood has told Colonel Murad – that Shani is involved in a love affair which is making him miserable. What Niazi will do is take Shani 'for a fuck'. There is a woman at a place he knows who is 'Southern Indian, petite and black as arseholes. She'll make your bones rattle so hard your ancestors will sit upright in their graves.'

A few minutes later Niazi parks in front of 'The Taj Massage Parlour' in Grant Road. Dad prepares to go in.

I have to say it is disconcerting to be entering a brothel with your father, particularly the sort of place which is described by Omar in his book as 'literally a flesh-market, the very pits, no one could sink any lower.' When it came to sex, in contrast to most of his brothers, who made no secret of their liking for women, my father was always rather conservative. He put safety and stability in the place of excitement. Clearly that hadn't always been the whole story.

CHAPTER FOUR

A cousin of mine, Nusrat, who lives in Karachi, has been visiting. I guess I see him every five years or so. He photographed Omar for the back jacket of *Once upon a Time*; he is also inside the book, as a baby, the first nephew.

The two of us go to visit a friend of his, a Pakistani diplomat. The Kashmir crisis has escalated once more, and I joke about the idea of its being a Pakistani who starts the Third World War. We meet at the Pakistan Embassy, where my father worked for thirty years and which I first visited aged four or five, for Christmas parties, wearing a jumper knitted by my grandmother and a policeman's helmet. When I didn't want to go to school, I'd accompany dad to work, sitting next to him at his desk, banging on a typewriter. Even later, at university, I'd call for dad at the Embassy and we'd go to a pub nearby for lunch.

The place hasn't changed: the miserable wallpaper, fraying carpets, and the photograph of Jinnah, now accompanied by Musharraf. There used to be an excellent canteen which was removed, my father once explained, because the tantalising cooking smells disturbed the Friday prayers of the other workers – they'd be thinking of kebabs and chapatis rather than Allah.

The diplomat is urbane and Western-educated; naturally, his children have been educated here. We have to go out for whisky. 'If I drink on the premises I will be sacked,' he says. Outside, on the steps, bearded Muslims in caps and salwar kameez hand out pamphlets about Islam and leaflets for political meetings at the mosque. British police with rifles walk in the road.

The diplomat tells me the 'nuclear' threat is showmanship. This is the only way both India and Pakistan can persuade powerful countries like America to help sort it out. The British may have gone, but there is still dependency. Nothing can be done without the 'big guns'.

The diplomat tells me that his ambition is to start a school in Pakistan. I say that I suppose education is something they'd need more of, along with electricity and clean water. He says yes, but before everything else his aim is to teach the kids 'the difference between right and wrong'. I'm surprised to hear this view, which is basically that of the Taliban, and want to say, 'As if anyone knows what that is.' I can't think of many people in the West who think of education as being primarily 'moral'. For us it's either information or the stimulation of natural curiosity. If I don't expect my children to be lectured morally at school, it is because I don't believe it'll be of any use to them. Our imperatives are no longer moral; they relate to success but are no less severe because of it. For us, being happy is more important than being good, and there isn't much relation between them.

It's been twenty years since I've visited Pakistan. As it's one of the world's most dangerous, and uncomfortable, countries, I'm not keen to return, although my curiosity as to what people are thinking has increased, particularly since the attacks on the World Trade Center. My cousin tells me how Karachi has 'improved' since I was last there. When I ask how, he says, 'We've got McDonald's now, and Kentucky Fried Chicken,' making it clear, as a lot of people in the Third World were already aware, that the aspects of the USA being exported were not education, culture, health and a tradition of dissent, but the worst, most degraded parts.

Nusrat works in PR but does some journalism too. However, he tells me he has to be 'careful'. If he wrote something critical of the government, he could be 'taken away' and stuck in a cell 'for a few days'. After, he would not be the same. He would not feel like writing or speaking out again. A man I have worked with, a Pakistani singer now living in Birmingham, has also been telling me about what a struggle it is in Pakistan to keep any sort of culture alive when the Moulvis attack music and the visual arts. He says they envisage a society in which there is no culture at all but only religious imperatives.

I ask my cousin whether he might have left Pakistan for the West as his uncles and some of our other cousins have done. The family has now more or less dispersed. One of my cousins is a doctor in Germany, and Omar's son lives in Dubai. Others live in New York and Canada.

Obviously Nusrat has thought about this often. If you're the dissenting type, or just want ordinary freedoms, you might have to make the difficult decision about whether to stay or leave. Both have their disadvantages. My cousin says he's afraid of working as a waiter or taxi-driver in the West. Not all Pakistani doctors, businessmen, computer gurus and accountants who leave are able to make it abroad. After all, it will always be 'less stressful' in Pakistan. Americans work too hard; Pakistanis drink tea and talk, as friends drift in and out of the offices. In the West conversation is less important. There his family's 'status' would count for nothing.

As we discuss this, I recall that Nusrat has turned up before in a book, as himself, in V. S. Naipaul's non-fiction account of the Islamic world, *Among the Believers*. 'Vidia always looks me up in Karachi,' Nusrat liked to say.

Returning to Naipaul's book, I see how 'Vidia' describes him: 'Nusrat was of mixed Punjab and Madras descent, so that in Pakistan he was half a native, half a mohajir or Indian Muslim stranger, half settled, half a man who felt that as a Pakistani and a Muslim he wasn't doing enough.' Then Naipaul quotes him as saying: 'We have to create an Islamic society. We cannot develop in the Western way. Development will come to us only with an Islamic society. It is what they tell us.'

Naipaul's book was published in 1981 and I read it in Karachi in 1982. (Seeing me reading it, Omar said, 'All Naipaul does is insult us.') Looking at the book again, I see that Nusrat discusses with Naipaul the same things as he talks about with me. But as he hasn't left Pakistan and now cannot face the consequences of such an 'exile', he can only worry about the other lives he might have led, which will, at the same time, seem alluring in comparison to his actual life. It's difficult, he says, not to feel like a 'poor cousin', someone left behind, compared to the 'sophisticates' who have got out.

Niazi, leading my father into the brothel, is compelled by the thought that the world is a dangerous place. The war is on Omar's mind too; in *Once upon a Time* he writes of the fear of India being bombed. For him, the fall of Singapore 'shatters' the myth of the white man's supremacy. In Bombay there is a 'brown-out' and rationing; posters are displayed urging people not to spread rumours. On the other hand, Omar writes about their district becoming a sort of Beverly Hills. Gulloo, the youngest brother, befriends the actor Dilip Kumar. Nearby there are dancers and starlets 'packing a lot of oomph'.

Then there are the returnees. Sattoo, one of the older brothers, is an Air Force officer. 'He had returned to India on a troopship and had to go round the Cape. They had docked at Cape Town but the Indian officers and men had not been allowed ashore in deference to South Africa's race laws. Sattoo led the protest and threatened a mutiny.'

Sattoo in RAF uniform

Like his father, Sattoo had come to dislike the Raj, having discovered, like other Indians in the armed forces, that the British were happy to have Indians die for them, but wouldn't admit them to their clubs. Not only that: Gandhi, in his *Autobiography*, writes of being forcibly removed from a first-class compartment in a South African train and compelled to ride in the van compartment. Later, on another train, he is beaten up. 'I saw that South Africa was no country for self-respecting Indians.'

The eldest Kureishi brother, Nasir, was seventeen years older than Omar and, during this period, was living in Calcutta, where he worked for the Indian Supplies Department. According to Omar, he and my father took the Calcutta Mail to visit him, a two-day journey 'across the vastness' of India. They saw the River Ganges for the first time but found, arriving at the station, men and women who looked like 'cadavers'. The children were unnaturally still, with bloated stomachs. These were not the conventional beggars of India. They were starving to death.

As children, father wanted us to eat, of course. How many family dramas are situated around what children will, and will not, put into their bodies? When dad got angry he said he would 'stuff the food down our throats'. The 'starving of India' seemed to be on TV a lot when I was a child. I guess we were looking at the first of many televised famines.

India was my father's country, and I can see that for him food – and what it was to eat or to feel hungry – had a different resonance than it did for us. We were also considering the contrast between our increasing plenty alongside the deprivation of a country the British had, until recently, total responsibility for. As consumption increased and people in the First World became more conscious of their bodies – all classes of people became fascinated by diets, nutrition and exercise – one of the purposes of the Third World was to serve as a reproach, to create a shadow of necessary guilt.

I remember thinking about this when I was writing *The Buddha of Suburbia*, particularly after visiting Rajneesh's commune in Poona. What was the place of the 'East' in the discourse of the 'West'? Both poverty and wisdom were being used for something. A benign religion such as Buddhism, along with the version of Hinduism people like George Harrison took up – less morally stringent than most Western religions – seemed to sit well with the increasingly frenzied capitalism of the West, creating a calm 'spiritual' space in the midst of social fragmentation and technological progress. If being a 'desiring machine', with its imperative to be successful at work, sex and play, becomes too stressful, there was, after a day's work, the possibility of spiritual peace and of 'oneness'.

There are, though, other forms of 'oneness'.

CHAPTER FIVE

In the brothel Shani is introduced to Lucy. Dad says, 'She was dusky, with fine-chiselled features. She wore a white cotton sari with a pink blouse. She walked gracefully, her hips swinging to give her bottom that oomph.' (There was obviously a lot of 'oomph' around in those days.) Niazi explains to her that his cousin Shani is a virgin and says, 'I want you to fuck the daylights out of him, Lucy.'

My father continues, 'Lucy took Shani into a big hall divided into cubicles. Inside them were long tables mounted on wooden crates and covered with white sheets. On them were placed green mattresses and two pillows.'

Complimenting him on his curls and pretty face, she undresses and washes him. Knitting her fingers around his penis, she tells him that sex is where 'man meets his Brahma. You go into a world of higher joy.' To help him control himself – dad is worried, as he puts it, about 'spilling the beans' – she recommends yogic breathing exercises. Perhaps this brothel was, then, the origin of my father's interest in yoga and breath control. When he died, I recall, he was doing his breathing exercises.

Father is very cheered by the whole event. There's no father, mother or brother – only him, the woman, and his pleasure without guilt or disgust. He never mentions the woman he is 'in love' with, Muni. In fact, he extols the virtues of prostitution as a marital aid, although, of course, he is not married and wouldn't be

61

for another twelve years. But Lucy has been such a good supplementary mother to him that he compares her to another Indian woman, Mother Teresa, who 'brings hope, comfort and help'. She sells him sex but also the idea of sex. If the scene begins with a boy being terrorized by his father, and the father, in turn, being humiliated by another man, Niazi, it concludes with a boy becoming potent and thinking about the world of pleasures ahead of him, away from his family.

Where does sex begin and end? Sex is often the memory of sex, as well as the fantasy and the anticipation. The sensuality of this scene reminds me of father's love of his own body: dad would display and discuss his muscles, thick neck, various scars, and the size of his stomach. As a child I would love to hang on his neck while he lifted me up; we would wrestle in the garden and race in the park, box and play badminton. Female in his narcissism, and with what I would describe as a 'Muslim gaudiness', he was forever fussing with his clothes, cuff-links, shoes, ties, colognes, talcum powder. He would shave in the morning and then shave again, in case he missed a couple of hairs. He would iron his own shirts and clean his own shoes. He would spend ages powdering, dressing, moisturising and worrying about his hair, which he always oiled. He loved mirrors and adored to be praised for his appearance. Then he would worry – because I wore an earring – about whether I was homosexual.

Where mother hid her body – it was private – dad loved to be touched by me. He wasn't much interested in my body and its burgeoning instincts: he had to be the one having pleasure. When he bathed, he took me with him. In the tiny bathroom I would wash his back, caress his head with oil, walk on his back, massage his legs and feet – an intimacy I adored, the child being made to feel privileged to fulfil what he knows should be the wife's role, and the father happily turned into the adored, pampered baby, again and again.

Omar describes Calcutta as being divided into two, a British part and a Bengali part. And, of course, India itself is about to be divided, as, indeed, is the Kureishi family. Omar says, 'India's own moment of truth was approaching.' Not far away, in Bombay's Shivaji Park, there were public meetings.

In my father's account the following happens: he is sitting on the balcony in the heat, considering what a calmer of fears and allayer of doubts Lucy is. She has taught him something useful about excitement, that it is something to be sustained rather than evacuated. Shani's recent sexual adventure has also been a triumph over his brother Mahmood, who still sleeps only with pictures of Betty Gable and Rita Hayworth.

But Shani's thoughts are interrupted by the sudden arrival of his friend Masood, last seen in the Irani restaurant. Masood tells Shani to come with him. 'There's a massive demo going on.' Nearby, in the park there are sirens, screams and the sound of gunfire. Congress demonstrators hold banners which say 'British Quit India. Down with British Imperialism.' 'A young man was shouting, "Comrades, we have burnt the Dadar police station and derailed the troop trains. Long live Jayaprakasn Narayan!"' (The Congress socialist party leader.)

The police attack the crowd with lathis and tear gas. A socialist worker tosses a petrol bomb at a police inspector, who burns to death in front of them. Shani ties the National flag to a tree. Suddenly he sees Muni, who is helping overturn a police van carrying demonstrators. A policeman is about to strike her over the head with his lathi, which might well kill her. Shani shouts a warning, picks up a stone and throws it at the policeman. Always an accurate shot, Shani's stone hits the policeman who collapses. Others in the crowd douse the man in petrol and set him on fire.

When the police begin to fire on the crowd, Shani drags Muni away to a safe place near the Irani restaurant. Shani then returns to the riot, seizes a lathi, whacks a policeman across the legs and releases Masood, who is about to be thrown in the back of a police van.

Shani returns to the waiting Muni. They watch as British troops with sten guns take up positions. Then the two of them flee to the beach where Muni puts her arm around Shani's waist. There is a lovely image: 'Two old men in white dhotis were bowing and sprinkling water on themselves, chanting in Sanskrit.'

She says, 'Don't you want to see me again?'

He does. They kiss and part.

So far in the course of this story, Shani has moved from one city to another, lost his virginity to a prostitute, been responsible for burning a policeman to death, saved a friend from arrest, and kissed the girl he is in love with. He is proud that he has taken part in India's freedom struggle, which is his own in more ways than one. And he has shown, in the written daydream we have just read, that he can be brave. He has saved his friend – the one with the name so similar to his brother's – and rescued the woman he believes he loves. They are in his debt at last.

He has rescued himself, too, but learned that being a hero cannot dissipate the suffering caused by desire. To want a woman is to bring on a host of other characters, to realise that other men will want her too, with whom one will have to compete. Even more obsessed with Muni, and with what she might offer him now she owes him so much, he cannot eat or sleep properly. This is partly India's fault: Indian parents guarded their daughters' virginity 'as though it was a pot of gold'. It would be impossible for a boy like him to visit Muni without a chaperone.

He discovers that this is exactly what his brother has done. Without telling Shani, Mahmood has gone to her house with the novel he promised. Not only that, Mahmood has taken Muni's mother some Yardley's powder and Pears soap, which he purchased in the Army and Navy Stores where he was familiar with the sales girl. (Along with books, soap seems to have become a form of currency for the Kureishi family.) According to Mahmood, Muni has even asked him to take her to see *Casablanca*. Just as he has always been closer to Bibi than Shani is, Mahmood has charmed both mother and daughter.

When Mahmood says he intends to give Muni lessons in how to ride a bike, adding that he 'might give her a ride too!', Shani explodes against the audacious, greedy, uninhibited brother. The two of them square up, about to fight. I wonder if there is about to be an apocalyptic confrontation between them. But Shani, reliving, it seems, his relationship with his father, already 'felt beaten, whipped. Cheated, double-crossed.'

Nevertheless, Muni does invite Shani over to the house; or rather, her mother does. Even more surprisingly, there, recovering from the riot, Shani finds Muni in bed. Above her hangs a large photograph of the aged George Bernard Shaw. As well as the soap which Mahmood has brought her, Shani notices the novel *Of Human Bondage*. (All the literary culture in dad's book is British.)

By now my father is frantic to know whether Muni will be his girl or not. Hasn't he saved her life? But her mother, chewing betel nuts and smelling of turmeric, brings in yet another man, Ashok. The mother explains, 'Shani, Ashok is engaged to Muni. They were engaged when Muni was three and Ashok was five. They'll get married next year.'

Shani can only reply, 'It's so nice to see that our medieval customs are still going strong. I thought child marriage was obsolete.'

Furious at his rejection – 'He was entering a world of cutthroats, sharp shooters, crooks, double-dealers, deceit and selfishness' – he returns home to find that his beloved grandmother, Nani, has died. 'She was the only person who truly loved him.'

Then something quite peculiar is said. Shani's mother Bibi is asking him to console her when Colonel Murad returns from his club, smelling of whisky. Seeing him, Bibi covers her face with her dupatta.

> It was over ten years since they had seen or spoken to each other. Colonel Murad still drank, and danced with Parsi women. It was really to save face, and Mahmood's insistence that they didn't do anything which would bring the family name into disrepute, which kept them together.

The more his mother mourns – and she is, inevitably, comforted by Mahmood – the more furious and resentful Shani becomes. She has neglected him, preferring to recite verses from the Koran; now she is weeping for herself.

I have said it seems odd that my father doesn't mention his parents' alienation from one another until the latter part of the book, where it appears almost as an afterthought. Ten years is a long time for a couple not to speak, and my father is only sixteen. However Bibi has already been shown to have been alienated from all of them. At the very least, my father would have been observing this mismatched marriage (which nonetheless produced twelve children) from close quarters. Whether they like it or not, children are always doing research into one marriage and discovering a great deal about disagreement, pleasure and the fate of love.

My father observed his parents' love, such as it was, as I observed his, and my children do mine, wondering what it might be this couple were doing together and what they might want from each other. And although there is a lot the children would miss, there is much they would pick up too, and who knows how this knowledge would work inside them, and what it might turn into, later.

For a time my parents' life together was, for me, the whole world. I did see that they never seemed to give one another much pleasure – they didn't seem to like being together – but the pain wasn't too intense either. I guess, then, that this suburban semi-sleep kept a lot of bad things away, both personal and political. The twentieth century might have been a disaster, but there were suburban enclaves in the West where nothing much occurred at all. As a rather protected child, I might not know what was being kept away, but I knew it was out there, so much so that the aftermath of leaving home was awful, a sort of mental illness.

One thing I had learned was that to make the marriage work, my parents divided the labour. My mother concentrated on my sister, and on her first love, watching TV. Like father, mother liked stories, soap operas in her case, which she watched every day, just as my maternal grandmother devoured scores of fat romantic novels. Mother was quiet and never spoke of herself, but when she did boast it was of her 'placidity', and she used the soaps as pacifiers – one good use of stories. Father didn't want a woman he had to compete with other men for. He was left to concentrate on me. He seemed to want to play all the roles: father, mother, brother, lover, friend, leaving little room for anyone else.

I guess I wondered a lot about what they were doing together, but it didn't seem to be something they considered. If I did suggest to dad that maybe he and mum might want to try living with other people, my father would say that it was cruel to leave women, as though without him they would have no resources at all. He would say he stayed with mum because I wouldn't like it if he left. He couldn't bring himself to say he stayed because he wanted to, or needed to, or that he liked it.

I did think, though, as I began to make my own sexual investigations, that what my parents had together wasn't something I wanted for myself. When I was twenty, in 1974, I wrote in my journal, 'My parents are morbid. Mother pities herself; she is already reconciled to any disaster.'

My own life with my own woman would be much better. There would be less routine and more excitement and unpredictability. That was the story I told myself.

Set a little later, the final chapter of my father's novel returns to a familiar, inescapable motif – my father's fear of his own father. Dad is returning to school after the holidays. During the break he has been concealing a letter from the British headmaster. Now he has to show it to Colonel Murad, who has to reply.

Father repeats the old fears: sweating, trembling, sleepless-ness. Shani has won cups, trophies, medals and certificates, his bowling has made the ground shake, but Colonel Murad has not responded with pride or love. The family might be obsessed with sport, and although cricket in India is an upper-class pre-occupation, the father cannot consider it a suitable occupation for his boys. Oddly, though, in the early 1950s, when Omar was playing cricket in Kent after his return from America, not far from where I was brought up, my grandfather did go to watch him play.

However, there is more of father's self-torment. 'Failure at sixteen! Life had hardly begun! What he needed was a father who would guide him.'

As father reluctantly makes his way to Colonel Murad we learn another peculiar thing: that his father's entire room is green. 'The ceiling, carpets, lamps, sofas – everything.' Apparently Colonel Murad believed that 'too many colours caused confusion'. On this occasion Colonel Murad is even wearing green, the symbol of natural life and fertility, but also of envy and death.

Shani reflects once more on the fact that Colonel Murad has been weakened, that his business is failing. He doesn't say much more about this, but my father does pop up in Omar's book in connection with the factory on a couple of occasions. After hav-ing passed his exams, Omar says, 'My brother Shannoo had failed in his Senior Cambridge examination. In the slang par-lance of the day, he had "plucked".'

According to Omar, my grandfather wanted my father to take over the failing soap factory, not unlike the way the young man in My Beautiful Laundrette takes over the old launderette, although in that case he was escaping his father's oppressive company, not joining him. Omar puts it this way, 'A very reluctant Shannoo started to accompany my father to the factory. He took along Thomas Mann's *The Magic Mountain*, which he was then reading.'

Omar and Shannoo are then sent to do a market survey in a town near Ahmedabad:

> It turned out to be a wonderful trip and we explored the small towns and villages, one journey was by camel. We returned home and reported that indeed the market looked promising. However, it was a period of shortages and, therefore, of the black market. My father decided to chuck it in, to his relief and to the even greater relief of Shannoo.

Father's book doesn't end so much as slow down and stop. I wonder whether there are any other pages missing, but doubt it. We discover that the letter which father has been concealing carries the news that he has been sacked as captain of the cricket team. He has refused to accept the racialist abuse of the white players. 'It was rare for an Indian to be in the team, rarer still to be captain. He had won the respect of the boys and teachers alike. Made Captain of English boys in an English School in Imperial India!'

Colonel Murad, with his army morals, demands obedience, while my father prefers conscience. Yet we are led to believe that, however grudgingly, the father approves of his own son. 'I didn't know, Shani, you had spunk in you. I'm pleasantly surprised.' As the schoolmaster's wife partners Colonel Murad at bridge, Colonel Murad agrees to use his influence to get Shani reinstated as cricket captain. 'We'll take it from there, okay?'

This, then, is the only place the book could possibly conclude. It is, despite everything, a happy ending.

It is here, for a while, that I lose my father. At the end of his account, and before I enter his life in the mid-50s, there is a ten-year gap. If I am to locate him again, it will have to be in Omar's second volume of autobiography, *As Time Goes By*. Before that, there is, at the end of Omar's first volume, something which startles me. You might recall that in dad's account he rescues not his brother Mahmood, but his similarly named friend Masood, from the riots. Masood is, I learn from Omar's book, the name of the brother who died in infancy in Tientsin, China, when the family was based there during the First World War. Although Omar, when he is in China, goes fruitlessly in search of the grave, he says, 'Neither my mother nor father ever spoke of him.'

Omar/Mahmood has the nerve to go to Muni with the gift of soap and a novel. Omar/Mahmood is less cautious than my father and enters the adult world with fewer fears. He has, as my father puts it, 'the gift of gab'. He believes he can charm people, that he is lovable, and that others will follow him. He seems to know that if his will is engaged there is little he cannot achieve. What a thing to believe; what a gift. My father, it seemed to me, was loveable too, in similar ways, yet he didn't believe in the efficacy of his gift and he couldn't get things done. Where does it come from then, the belief that one can make a difference to others, that one can mean something in their lives?

Indeed, at this young age, Omar is thinking of making films himself, which surprises me. I had no idea there was such a precedent in the family. Yet I began writing my first film, *My*

Beautiful Laundrette, while staying in Karachi in the early 80s. I'd gone there at Omar's instigation, to visit him, Sattoo and my cousins. The film was, then, a combination of scenes which were taking place across the courtyard from my room, transposed to Britain, and mixed in with elements from my past.

Thinking about it now, I am aware that my film concerns two brothers, one 'useless', the other 'effective', between whom the young hero moves. With the 'useless' brother, played by Roshen Seth, the son is prop and nursemaid; the father has no one but him. The story begins to gather speed when the 'effective' brother, played by Saeed Jaffrey, leads the boy into a sexualised, semi-criminal, dangerous world apart from the father. In *The Buddha of Suburbia*, too, I sexualised the family, turning them on, putting desire at the centre of the family. In my version they were all looking for something, not just waiting. This was because the waiting at home had seemed interminable; and while we were waiting, we were writing, since there was nothing else to do.

In Bombay Omar began to work for Zabak, one of the two brothers I never met. Running a movie magazine called *Sound*, Zabak was, according to Omar, something of a bohemian who 'lived on the edge'. I can recall my father, always more cautious, describing Zabak as a brilliant journalist who became a tragic alcoholic, drinking the roughest, cheapest hooch, and eventually destroying himself, isolated from the family in Japan.

Long before this, and using Zabak's office as a base, Omar decided to begin his own magazine, which he would call *Appeal*, a 'non-political magazine of general interest'. My father was the 'business editor'. Omar soon realised that such work was what, passionately, he wanted to do. His father approved, too. Soon there was a first issue, which my grandfather took to his club to read. The whole thing made Omar intensely happy.

But the exodus of Muslims from India was about to begin, and not only was the country about to be divided, it was on the verge of civil war. Omar had to work out where and how he would live. Two brothers were still in London, Achoo at the LSE. But Sattoo, the admired elder brother who'd been a pilot, had returned to begin an airline. Omar asks, 'Would we migrate to Pakistan as a whole family or would we opt to stay in Bombay? Or would we disperse?'

There were to be only two issues of *Appeal*. In Indian epics the heroic Prince has to experience exile – to be separated from the mother – before he can return as a man. Omar was offered a place at the University of Southern California, in the School of Cinema. Tootoo was already in America and Omar's close schoolfriend, Zulfikar Bhutto, was going too.

But there were worries. If they were 'natives' in India, in America there was the 'race question', which had been brought to their attention by what they knew of Paul Robeson. Another serious drawback was the fact that cricket was not played in Los Angeles. For Omar, the time of Colonel Kureishi's XI was important; the whole family seemed at one then. Mother and father may not have been speaking, and there might have been twenty-two years' difference between the first child and the last, but there was an intimacy between them all which appeared indestructible. Now Omar seemed aware that although he was able to get out, the family he was leaving behind were about to live through a terrible conflict.

My father, as usual, went to see him off.

CHAPTER SIX

On the cover of the second volume of Omar's autobiography is an American flag and three photographs: Omar and Bob Hope; Omar in a bow tie, debating; and the third, handsome Omar in an open-necked shirt, with a woman who seems pleased to see him. He was in America in August 1947 when the Union Jack was lowered in Karachi and he remarks, with some pride, 'We had our own homeland.'

Omar with Bob Hope

Omar makes it clear that the end of colonialism is difficult for everyone. After America, where will he go? To Pakistan? 'Would I be an outsider? I had, after all, never even visited Karachi and had not lived in any part of what was now Pakistan.'

Despite these worries, this volume, which is full of pleasure and jokes, has the irreverent, gossipy tone of the Kureishi family when they're together, minus the baiting or belittling. However, going to America was a big trip for someone barely into their twenties. In those days these were considerable emotional journeys. In 1950, when V. S. Naipaul left Trinidad for London, it was six years before he saw his family again and he writes, 'To go abroad could be to fracture one's life.'

Yet along with his brother Tootoo and Zulfikar Bhutto (who vociferously abhors the creation of Israel and has a violent 'altercation' with a Jewish student), Omar debated, explored, and had girlfriends. He even appeared as an extra in the MGM version of *Kim*. More significantly, Omar broadcast on radio for the first time. He joined in with a curiosity and enthusiasm I'd never have managed myself. The writing expresses a joy which my father seems incapable of. Omar writes, 'The trophies I was winning [for debating] were beginning to clutter up my room.'

My father, I had thought, was still in India. This is a period I'm interested in, the first time he had been at home without his brother for an extended interval. Then I read, 'My brother Shannoo had left for Glasgow to study Marine Engineering. Fat chance he had of beoming a marine engineer. He had wanted to be a writer.'

'By and by the ship arrives and docks in Southampton,' wrote Tagore in 1879. This was a journey, then, not unknown to Indians. My father had left with little idea when he would see his home and parents again, or whether he would return at all. As a teenager, when playing truant from school, I would, when my mother came home from work at lunchtime, hide out in the attic reading Donleavy's *The Ginger Man* by torchlight. My father's trunk, made in India, covered in exotic labels, would dominate the little room. He told me several times how homesick he had been on this trip from Bombay to Southampton, and

Shannoo in Paris

how, coming through the Suez Canal, he had to be persuaded not to jump ship and return to his parents.

My father was in London, having given up the idea of becoming a marine engineer, when Omar left America and came to England for the first time. Omar was to join Colonel Kureishi, my father and Achoo, for Sattoo's lung operation, after he had contracted TB. Sattoo had been in the US buying aircraft for the new national airline, PIA, 'which will provide the vital link between the two wings of the country'. But he had to have a lung removed.

My father, accompanied by Achoo and my grandfather, met Omar at the station. For Omar, compared to California, England was a 'damp despondancy'. After the debacle of the soap factory, my grandfather seemed to have retired, moved to England and separated from Bibi. I know little about this, but I think he was having an affair with a woman who lived in Hastings. (Apparently it was his 'affairs' which stood in the way of his becoming a general.)

While Sattoo was in hospital, Colonel Kureishi visited every ay. In this account my grandfather does not seem like a neglectful or indifferent father, though having left his work, wife and country, he can't have had much else to do. Nonetheless, it must have been this devotion to at least some of his sons, the older ones perhaps, which drove dad crazy, that made him feel particularly excluded.

I have discovered a short story by my father which seems to piquantly illustrate dad's inability to reach Colonel Murad. Called 'A Ride in the Rickshaw' and set in dad's birthplace, Madras, it concerns Ramu, a rickshaw-wallah, taking a fat, older man – described as looking like the actor Sydney Greenstreet – about the city. The rickshaw puller is ill and is trying to save money in order to see a doctor. All day the wealthy man reclines in the rickshaw reading a paper with the headline 'Singapore Falls'. The story ends with the passenger going into a hotel which Ramu is forbidden to enter. There the man disappears without paying the fare. My father always uses realism as his preferred form; he disliked the arts being 'experimental', as though other ways of writing implied other ways of living. But this work becomes almost surreal – or Eastern European – in its political incisiveness and grotesque physicality, as you are made to contemplate the image of a skinny, dying Indian dragging a bloated body past the beggars of the boiling, colonised city. Whenever I read it, I think of rewriting it as a fable – and now, I guess, I have.

While Sattoo was recovering from his operation, the Kureishis, such as they were, became the only Asian family in St Leonards, just outside Hastings, Sussex. Omar describes the Sussex pubs, cricket pavilions and buses of 1950s England, an area I've always enjoyed reading about, in *Brighton Rock* and, particularly, in Patrick Hamilton's *Hangover Square*.

After so long in America, Omar took up cricket again and discovered that as far as this sport was concerned, England's class system resembled the Hindu caste system. There were still 'gentlemen' and 'players' (those who earned their living as sportsmen). 'On the score card, these players were called by name whereas the gentlemen had the prefix "Mister". There was a separate dressing room for them and they would enter the field from a different gate.'

Omar got to know his elder brother, Achoo, who introduced him to modern poetry and literature – in the form of Eliot and Joyce, whom they would discuss in country pubs. Achoo was in a similar position to Omar – drifting, while hoping to find out how he should live his life. They never quite know what they should be doing, these over-educated and somewhat Chekhovian Kureishi boys – Chekhovian in their drift and futility – as though there was indeed something important they ought to be discovering, while lesser things shouldn't distract them. They always seem too intelligent, or grand, for the situation they find themselves in, as though the world will always drag them down, rather than lift them up. There's a sense of waste in their lives, which won't leave them alone.

When, finally, Omar decided to go to Pakistan and restart his life, my father was, of course, at Victoria Station to see him off. By now dad had become a clerk in the Embassy, occupying a little room overlooking Lowndes Square in Knightsbridge in which there was a desk, a chair, a filing cabinet and a couple of big typewriters. The Embassy of the new country hadn't been long established; many of the jobs were occupied by English people. I suspect dad took the clerk's position as a temporary post, in order to pay his rent. I can remember hearing about dad's colleagues coming and going, but this was the only job dad was to have. Years before, Bibi's mother Nani had said to Omar, 'May God make you a Deputy Collector.' Omar calls this 'pukka employment'. Pukka employment was what my father had found, Colonel Murad's regime at home having been replaced by what we called in the 60s 'the system'.

Before Omar left, the two brothers had a last talk. Omar writes: 'Shannoo told me he was working on a novel but not getting too far with it. I gave him the standard "bourgeois" reply which was that he should complete his studies. In his school and college days he had been a brilliant cricketer but had not distinguished himself in the classroom.'

After they married, dad moved in with mother and her parents in the suburb of Bromley, in Kent, where my mother had always lived. My first memories are of the little corner shop we had, where mum worked until my sister was born. But it was cramped, and in 1958, when I was four, we moved into the house which would be my only family home. It was nothing like any of the houses my father had grown up in. There were two bedrooms upstairs and two rooms downstairs, with a 'box-room' at the side, which became a dining room. It was quiet and there was a garden, which my bedroom overlooked. My sister and I slept at the back, my parents at the front, and my grandparents downstairs. The shops were about ten minutes' walk away. The road itself was a cul-de-sac and was situated next to a park where I played football and cricket. I learned to smoke in the sheds; it was where I touched a girl's body for the first time.

79

The winters were freezing: mother getting up early to light the coal fire, all of us crammed into the only warm room in the house, watching sit-coms, Dickens adaptations and Charlie Chaplin and Laurel and Hardy films on TV. At night the bed would be frozen; mother would give us a hot-water bottle and an apple; my fingers would stick to the plastic covers on the library books. In the morning, on the way to school, there was the fog.

Once I could ride a bicycle, I had a freedom never possible for my children, here in the city. My father, who moved a lot in his youth and made one big journey – to England – never wanted to move house again. He loved the suburbs, where he said he had everything he needed. To insult the suburbs was to insult him: he took it personally.

In terms of worldly success, my father did less well than almost all the other brothers. He was in a low-status job with a small income. He complained about how much it bored him, and how stuck he felt. It seemed to mystify him, and he made it mystify us, not only how someone like him ended up there, but how he came to believe it was the only life possible for him. When it became hard going, he liked to represent himself as trapped. Without a family, he liked to suggest, it would have been different.

If one of the complaints about Asians was that we didn't join in, or wouldn't integrate – as though difference is unbearable, or that people can only like those who are the same as them – this couldn't be said of my father. Dad never attempted to become an Englishman; that was impossible. But he did join in the English way of life.

It had been painful for my father to see the family furniture sold off in Poona. By the mid-60s the idea of the consumer society had arrived in the London suburbs. Cheap and plentiful household goods were becoming a form of self-definition for everyone. I can remember our first television, fridge and washing machine. When the TV arrived, we and the neighbours would gather round on hard chairs, as though we were at the theatre, waiting for it to warm up, and then begin. Snobbery had been democratised; disposability was the keyword. If your furniture bored you, you threw it away. By the 1980s disposability had permeated everything, including love.

On Saturday mornings, we would shop in Bromley High Street for new furniture, about which my parents would argue furiously, while I hung around, waiting to be taken to the library and then to the Wimpy Bar for hamburgers and icecream. There were a succession of brash carpets, which later, when I became craftily knowing, I liked to characterise as their 'Bridget Riley phase'; G-plan coffee tables and chipboard bookshelves followed. In the collection of my father's expressions I keep there's a phrase which sums it up: 'They were shopping madly on tick!'

More extraordinarily, like the other men in the area, my father decided to take up DIY. Not much had been done to these houses since the war. Some of them still had outside toilets. However, unlike the other men, my father had done nothing like this before. I remember him deciding, somewhat arbitrarily, to 'redo' the ceilings. He would glue polystyrene tiles to the ceilings of some of the rooms. He'd cut these tiles unevenly and so they never fitted; little bits of white polystyrene stuck to the curtains and carpets for months, as father, secured at the legs by mother and me, stood on a chair trying to stick this stuff up. In the evenings, as we watched *Dad's Army* or other TV comedies, these tiles would flutter down, leaving ugly glue patches on the ceiling. Whether father was 'passing' or not, I didn't know; nor did he. What he did emerged as parody, making our lives seem ridiculous, as though there was no seriousness possible.

Bits of India, or rather, the bits that existed in his family, stuck to dad. They were mostly cultural: cricket, books, music, politics. But dad did teach himself to cook well. When he prepared curry, he'd begin in the morning and spend all day in the kitchen. It was a sort of Zen exercise in patience. Father had, of course, a love and knowledge of sport in common with the local men. In the park dad would organise cricket matches with the local boys; he'd talk to them about their lives and problems; he'd encourage them; I'd feel jealous. The Oedipal fears and terrors he describes in his novel appear to have passed, as Freud says they should inevitably do, in later life; or he seems to have found a way to live in which they didn't disturb him.

From the child's point of view, the parents apparently spend their time trying to earn a living and run the house; the rest of their energy is spent in making numerous decisions: negotiating, disputing, arguing, struggling to reach agreement, or trying to disagree amicably. There appears to be little pleasure in this, but the parents convince the child that this is the only way for them to survive. The child can come to believe it is his or her job to cheer them up.

Despite this, my parents had enough in common, both wanting to lead a controlled, peaceful life, following the suburban model of contented housewife, heterosexual father at work, and children learning well at school. This was a paradigm we saw often on television, in British sit-coms, as well as in *I Love Lucy*,

The Dick Van Dyke Show and *Bewitched*. This wasn't the version which Omar would have had much contact with in America. It was, though, a world I recognised, later, in John Cheever's stories, though in his rendition it is more affluent. He puts the aspiration pertinently in 'The Country Husband': 'The people in the Farquarsons' living room seemed united in their tacit claim that there had been no past, no war – that there was no danger or trouble in the world.' But Cheever was amused by the psychic cost of such contentment. After falling for the young baby-sitter, the protagonist visits a psychiatrist to whom he announces, fatefully, 'I'm in love, Dr Herzog.' Cheever's characters are always falling in love inappropriately; that is their grace and their downfall.

Cheever makes it clear that complacency is impossible and, anyway, undesirable. The attempt to make an entirely safe environment – coffee without caffeine, war without killing, sex without contact – can only diminish life. A world in which people can't die is a world in which people can't live. What else is there, apart from passion and its vicissitudes?

A few years ago I was asked to speak to a group of business students about the point of culture. They and I were looking at one another with some bewilderment when someone said, 'Do we really need art?' I thought of the suburbs and the misuse of art and culture as social differentiation – snobbery – and of their association with pretentiousness and showing off, as Eva in *The Buddha of Suburbia* uses them. Yet this was not the norm. Most people participate in some kind of communal art: they dance, sing, play instruments, take photographs, garden, tell stories. Almost everything we do has some aesthetic dimension. People prefer beauty to ugliness. However, culture and sensual abandon can seem like close associates. As religious fundamentalists know, art and the body are inextricable. Culture attacks all certainties, and cultural deprivation is a form of deliberate poverty. Father, with his regular writing and determination to get published was, at least, keeping some form of expression alive.

Like me, dad may have been a failure at school, but he took his reading seriously; he knew his way around literature, politics and sport. And, despite his determination to join in, dad was always trying to find time to write, which would prove his singularity. His life was partly formed by his rejection at the hands of various publishers. He sent his books out and they would be returned; he'd rewrite them and they'd come back again. Hope; despair; renewal. Occasionally, father would threaten to give up trying to be a writer. From his point of view this would be a disaster, a kind of suicide. A couple of days later he'd be back at his desk with a new idea. Once, he said he wanted to continue because he didn't want me to see him be defeated.

It must have perplexed mother – this man's attempt to do something at which he had no success, while not giving up and never accepting he was doing it for fun, as a hobby, but continuing to believe that it would become his profession and identity. Let's suppose that all the time the woman, my mother, knew that the man was not being realistic. From her point of view, if he forfeited his fantasies their life would be fuller; writing divided him from her, and from the life she wanted them to have together. But how do you persuade someone to give up their deepest fantasies? Suppose it were true, as it seemed to be for father, that the 'real' world wasn't the mundane reality of trains, umbrellas, routine, conversations at bus stops, but a world which existed at the level of fantasy, in the daily dream rather than in waking life? Dad lived the perfect life, then, wherein his fantasies, coalesced around writing, could be expressed in his books. Father's real life could continue to exist in the future, when he would become a writer. Father lived one life but wished he could live another – let's call it a parallel life, which was always beyond him, but was the paradise which he would, one day, enter. We would follow him, of course. In that sense it was a joint project, though we had no choice in the matter. Meanwhile, we waited. The ironic thing is that if father had really been persuaded to give up his art – or, worse, if he had succeeded at it – he might have succumbed to mental illness; his writing and perhaps its very failure kept him going and hoping, kept chaos and anxiety away.

Of course the puzzle of books, what they did and the satisfaction they provided, had always been at the centre of the family. Two of my father's older brothers, Abo and Achoo, both of whom had spent the war in London, were particularly academic. Abo was in Karachi, married to an important Pakistani poet and academic, Maki Kureishi; Achoo, after studying Law, was in a Somerset village, running a school for autistic children. Achoo was much older than my father and they hadn't known each other well as children, but now his daughter was eighteen months younger than me; we were firm friends and enemies. Being the offspring of a child psychologist, she was far less restrained and much more self-destructive than me. We had both suffered similar problems at school, and had been devastated in ways we didn't understand by racism.

Every summer we'd drive to Somerset to stay for a while. The Kureishi siblings, though scattered, were always in touch, and usually alive in one another's minds. Achoo's flat was a few miles from Evelyn Waugh's house. (Achoo met him once, locally, and offered him his hand; Waugh – a writer I still admire for his prose – offered not his hand but a finger.) Achoo's booklined study, with its sofas, music and pictures, was my favourite place. There he would read Chaucer, Milton, Shakespeare, Russell and Orwell, going through them like a student reading primers, making notes, underlining. We'd listen to scratchy recordings of Beethoven and of Gielgud's *Hamlet*, the ghost making hideous noises. The library atmosphere of hard-working calm was one I wanted.

I preferred sitting with him to being with other kids. Achoo was not unlike some of Bellow's or Singer's characters, an immigrant obsessed with self-education and scholarship, while remaining otherworldly, not quite connected to what was going on, using books as a barrier between himself and reality. My father was always urging Achoo to write, which annoyed him; like some of the other elder brothers, he thought my father was a little crazy with this writing stuff. Achoo thought that to be a writer one had to know things, like Bertrand Russell or Orwell, or be close to nature, like the romantics or D. H. Lawrence.

One summer, I must have been fourteen, I was sent to Achoo as I was hopeless at maths; I didn't get along with my mother either. My uncle recognised there was some connection between these two failures. As Achoo discussed maths with me, I'd look around the room. Although I knew the names of most novelists, Achoo had books by writers I'd never heard of: Melanie Klein, Anna Freud, Piaget, A. S. Neill and Winnicott.

He talked to me about a new area of investigation, saying this was something which hadn't been done before: the analysis of children and the notion of their development. He told stories about the difficult children at his school – about their violence, muteness and inability to learn – and their strange behaviour, which covered a black hole of despair. The intention was to listen to them, rather than have them shut up. He said their seemingly 'mad' attitudes made sense. The aim, though, via loving education, was to replace activity with speaking. This was, of course, before the 'therapy' culture we now inhabit, and the language of self-disclosure which accompanies it. The most important things were hidden then, and literature was the only place you could find them. But literature itself was a hard code for a young person to break. Achoo insisted, however, that if his pupils wanted to learn something they should be able to come to him, and he'd either teach them himself, or help them find books or a teacher.

Just being the sort of man he was taught me a lot. Then he said this astonishing thing. Sometimes my uncle hypnotised me, but on this occasion he was talking, saying that surely I'd noticed how my mother had 'a beautiful smile and a lovely singing voice'. He told me that I wanted to make love to my mother and kill my father. Anticipating my protest, he said all men, including him, had felt like this; surely I'd noticed that literature was full of such desires? The play *Hamlet*, for instance, had this structure. He could remember, he continued, wanting to have sex with his mother. I shut my eyes, trying not to think of such a thing. When I opened them again I saw that his were full of tears. 'If only I could see her again,' he said. 'Too many of us brothers went away and never went back. We wanted her, she wanted us, but we were not there.'

This shocked me in the best way: I was intrigued, fascinated. That family life was Oedipal seemed a wild thing for an educated adult to say, more improbable than anything I'd heard from my friends or in pop music. It was as though, before this, I had seen the mad and the sane in quite different categories, even though literature teaches us that this is clearly not the case. But if the sane were also mad, how did we live with this? Such ideas were something I wanted to know more about. Where were they written down?

Behind my uncle's head, in the hardback Hogarth edition, was the complete Freud, which had just been translated. Achoo's room was full of oriental knick-knacks; Freud's couch, of course, was draped in an oriental rug. Not that anything in Freud made any sense to me when I looked at it later. Achoo went on to say that what was kindly referred to as civilisation was always frustrating. Men and women were at their happiest when they were most like the animals they had been, a long time ago. This was even more puzzling: my father wanted me to be a writer but my uncle wanted me to be an animal. He believed his book learning had done little for him, yet it was partly that which I loved about him.

CHAPTER SEVEN

It was when Omar went to Pakistan that his and my father's lives seemed to diverge for good. Omar writes, 'I had left India, an old country, in June 1947, and had returned to Pakistan, a new country, in November 1953.'

This journey is described in Omar's third volume of autobiography, *Home to Pakistan*, where he went to join most of the other Kureishis, who had by then moved to Karachi, a city he did not know. But he was enthusiastic. 'I had come to Pakistan by choice, not for what the country could do for me but what I could do for the country. There was in the early Pakistan pioneer something of the Pilgrim Father who had arrived in the United States on the *Mayflower*, a certainty of belief and a measure of arrogance, common to all do-gooders.'

He worked as a journalist for the *Karachi Times* and then became a cricket commentator. Before television, and when there was little sport in the newspapers, the ball-by-ball radio commentary was listened to by millions, a five-day battlefield narrative with the commentators as Greek chorus. Even those who didn't speak English listened. At first, in Sattoo's house, Omar shared a room with Bibi, his mother, who wasn't able to understand what he was saying on the radio, but could tell by the tone of his voice how the team was doing.

Omar became a celebrity; his name, along with those of the players, was known by everyone. Cricket, rather than politicians or culture, carried the pride, hope and ambition of the fledgling nation. The politicians and generals were already more forgettable.

In a nascent Third World country, sport can represent a public affirmation and focus for patriotism. Leon Trotsky told C. L. R. James that spectator sport was a substitute for political action. James, being more sophisticated, saw cricket as part of the 'historical movement' of the times, deeply intertwined with the society. Certainly, two of the most illuminating and educational crises of my childhood concerned sport and politics, the one leading to some knowledge about the other. The case of Muhammed Ali and his conscription clash with the US government over the Vietnam war was one. The second, and more important for me – an issue where I saw that sport was no more exempt from race politics than was sex – was the case of Basil D'Oliviera.

D'Oliviera was a talented mixed-race South African all-rounder who'd had a Catholic education. As a 'coloured' he was unable to represent his country as a professional player because of the race laws. Brought to England by the mellifluous-voiced cricket journalist John Arlott – Omar's radio mentor – he was signed up as a professional by Worcestershire. In 1968, at the age of thirty-five, D'Oliviera was refused permission, even as an England cricketer, to play in South Africa, leading to the cancellation of the tour. The South African Prime Minister John Vorster said, 'It's not the England team, it's the team of the anti-apartheid movement.' After an outcry and much debate about the place of politics in sport, sporting links between the two countries were severed until the release of Nelson Mandela.

For Trotsky, political action was the real thing; everything else was a sort of sublimation. Culture and sport were surplus to the essential need to change society. Certainly, it seems reasonable to feel guilty about loving sport and art in a way it doesn't about loving one's country or one's work. Once again pleasure is problematical. C. L. R. James, however, understood the complexity of cricket. He saw it as an art, as an aesthetic spectacle, and he compared cricketers, doing something both dangerous and dignified at the highest level and in front of massive crowds, to performers like Menuhin and Gielgud.

Omar had never been under any illusion about the intersection of sport, culture and politics. Having been the first Pakistani journalist to visit the People's Republic of China, where he interviewed Chou En-Lai, he then took the Pakistan cricket team to Kenya and even played for them, alongside Hanif Mohammed, the world's best batsman. However, after the *Karachi Times* was taken over by the government and martial law was imposed – not for the last time – Omar began to feel pessimistic about the future of Pakistan. In Bombay 'they were friends with Hindus, Parsis, Anglo-Indians and Jews'. Karachi was not mixed in this way, and 'dissent was becoming dangerous'.

If there was to be any form of democracy in the foreseeable future, then there had to be some belief in education – education as a training in independent, critical thought, rather than as rote learning. But the government of Pakistan, corrupt already, couldn't see this as a priority. As Nusrat's diplomatic friend said, education was about 'right and wrong', ultimately a form of moral coercion. Otherwise, knowledge could be subversive, it might show alternative lives. At the very least Omar had realised something important in China: that he was not a communist. Besides, when 'designing' Pakistan, Jinnah had envisaged a racially and religiously mixed society. It would be neither socialist nor a theocracy. 'He did not want religion to be the business of the state.' However, Pakistan's tragedy was that it could not make up its mind what it wanted to be and didn't have time to find out. Meanwhile it was becoming corrupt and elitist.

The third volume of Omar's autobiography stops at the end of the 1950s, and although he is not a pessimistic person, he seems already disillusioned with the prospects of his new homeland. He does say something significant, almost in passing, about the sort of society he sees emerging, a way between communism and liberal democracy adopted by the schoolfriend of Omar and my father, Zulfikar Bhutto: 'I wanted Islam to be the guiding star, its moral direction . . . its social philosophy, its dynamic message of the dignity and equality of all.'

To read this shocks me; when I think about it, I lose my bearings. I'd never imagined a liberal and literary man finding a combination of social hope and justice in a religion which, for me, can only seem a betrayal of our family's values. It is inevitable that you would break with your family in different places and at different times. But for us to be divided on this particular point – Islam – is to be faced with more questions than answers.

CHAPTER EIGHT

The sun was shining this morning, and we went to the second-hand book shop in Gloucester Road, which we visit often on Sundays. The house is filling up with books; one more won't make any difference. My girlfriend Monique and our five-year-old, Kier, waited in the coffee shop next door, him on a high stool, drawing in his notebook. After, we went to Hyde Park, Kier on his bicycle, to see the Peter Pan statue. He climbed it, and hid in the bushes. I had bought the *Selected Poems* of William Carlos Williams.

When I find myself becoming impatient with the students I teach, I write poetry, and then I know the fumbling clumsiness, the inadequacy, the pain of incapability, because I am unable to write a poetic line which sounds like me. For me, poetry is more sensual than prose. It shoves the story out of the way, as well as the laborious machinery of the novel – plot, numerous characters, setting – leaving just the moment: only the local. If I can write a story which seems more like a poem than a piece of prose, I am delighted. I like the conversational style of Williams and particularly of Frank O'Hara – his ability to write the everyday, and concentrate it. O'Hara wrote poems during his lunch break at the Museum of Modern Art. 'Mothers of America/ Let your kids go to the movies!/ Get them out of the house so they won't know what you're up to.'

When you look at a work of art which fails to satisfy you,

you realise how demanding you are, that there's something missing from your life. Luckily, some poems make you love things more, and what can be more important?

I am beginning to realise how apprehensive I am about writing this book and the feelings it gives me, and keeps giving me, about my father. O'Hara's lines about mothers finding pleasure without their kids make me think, for reasons I don't understand, how obvious it is that dad should have married Muni, at least for a while. He both knew, and refused to know, how interested she was in him, much more than in his brother. She wanted to see how persistent he could be. But he was persistent only with the writing, ducking out of anything else difficult, fearing he couldn't bear it.

And me? What sort of remark have I just made? What have I been doing, opening up father like this, examining, diagnosing, operating on him, so that this work feels like a cross between love-making and an autopsy? I have to say I don't know what sort of book I am making here, as I spin my words out of his words, stories out of other stories. It feels more like a pot into which I am stirring almost everything that occurs to me. Anyhow, for a month I haven't had the nerve to look at this material. I feel guilty about what I am doing to the family. By what right can I do this? Who does father, or anyone, belong to? Yet I am still curious about this method, and want to continue. How can plain curiosity be unkind?

Having survived this immersion in my father's body, this reconnection with my family's past, I spend half a day in my basement, rifling through the damp boxes which constitute my 'archive'. I want more. As St Augustine wrote about one of his own works, 'In writing this book I have learned many things I did not know.'

94

Among the manuscripts, letters and photographs I unearth – many of which are wet and ruined – I discover another of my father's novels, along with a play, 'Grocer and Son'. The novel, 'The Redundant Man', I do in fact remember leafing through before, in the early 80s. Omar was on a binge in London and taking only ice-cream and vodka, a combination I would recommend. Reclining unshaven in bed in a darkened room in South Kensington, with smears of dried blood on his face, he was given a copy by dad. 'It's about him,' Omar said to me later, with some sadness. Omar wasn't always so measured. Sometimes, as I sat there listening to his stories – he didn't get out of bed for four months, but I'd developed an assiduous bedside manner, having had so much practice with dad – he'd turn his attention to me and say, 'How come you turned out to be such a twerp and cunt?' 'Must be my family background,' I'd say. Reply: 'Smartarse, too.'

At the same time he was trying to persuade me to write a movie with him. I was already beginning to think about *My Beautiful Laundrette* and wrote in my diary, 'Had the idea of writing a two-hander for Pakistani or Indian actors. There could be a son in it.' Omar talked about wanting to do something about the immigrant 'as comedian, like Charlie Chaplin'. While I liked the idea of creating recognisable and amusing contemporary characters, this wasn't quite it; his idea wasn't right for me. Even as we talked, Omar still had style. When I wanted to eat, he had the food sent over in a taxi from a Mayfair restaurant, a turbanned lackey in a gold-braided uniform unpacking it for me. On one of these occasions, dad and I turned up proudly with a copy of the *Guardian*, in which I was mentioned in a piece by Rushdie, whose family lived a few streets away from us in Karachi. A few minutes later Omar's son arrived with a copy of the same day's *Guardian*, in which he was also mentioned. Seeing this son, so similar to me, dad reminded me of the way in which I really was unique: 'Never forget how lucky you are that I'm your father.'

Dad worked on 'The Redundant Man' for several years. I can recall clumsily giving dad advice about it, and feeling bad after, for being hard on him, even as he blamed me for its failure to get published. 'But you are knowing all these damn people, yaar,' he'd say. He put us on the same level: writers – almost brothers – together, with neither of us more talented than the other.

The novel seems to be one he wrote before 'An Indian Adolescence', and it is different in tone and style. If I had read it first, I doubt whether I would have wanted to persist with this project. 'An Indian Adolescence' is written from the point of view of a child in conflict with his parents, while 'The Redundant Man' is partly about a father in conflict with his children. Whereas 'An Indian Adolescence' is a book for others – one which could have been cut, reshaped and published – this one seems like father expressing his desperation without any outside referent. It is an uncontrolled book, written by someone railing against (a familiar) failure and 'uselessness', for which they cannot quite locate the reason or source. If the novel, with its grotesques, disguises and longeurs, is read as a dream, it is a revealing one.

Set during the Thatcher 'reorganisations' of the early 80s, when unemployment was high and the idea which life in the suburbs was built around – that people would have jobs for life – was breaking down, 'A Redundant Man' concerns Yusef, a fifty-year-old Pakistani man in a job not unlike my father's. When Yusef is made redundant, he feels he has been cruelly used. Although dad himself was not made redundant – others around him were – it could easily have been a release he wished for.

The scenes with Yusef's 'superiors', as the clerk begs to be retained – scenes set, it appears, in the room I visited with Nusrat – are long, repetitive and sadistic. In the pointless intimidation and endless office procedures, they remind me of *The Trial*, as well of the confrontations with Colonel Murad in 'An Indian Adolescence'. Dad must have felt badly bullied by his brothers, as his mother prayed to Allah and his father danced with Parsi girls. My father writes of his boss, 'He had crushed me like some despicable insect. Stripped me of all human dignity. Left me ashamed of my nakedness. I clenched my fists and gnashed my teeth. But the rage was temporary, that of an impotent man.'

Dad's ambivalence about authority and about being bullied wasn't concentrated exclusively on Omar. At the end of his life, when I was working in the theatre, dad went alone to visit Achoo, knowing it was the last time they would see each other. It was quite a trip for dad, this man who didn't like travelling. Like dad, Achoo had been sick for years; he had had heart failure. While there, dad would ring me, asking whether I 'required' him in London. He complained that Achoo was raving and being nasty to him but that he couldn't think of an excuse to leave, as though he were mesmerised. He wanted me to get him out of there.

At the insistence of mother and I, dad did try to find other work. We believed a change would do him good. In 'The

97

Redundant Man' Yusef applies, as my father did, for a clerical job with the police. He is told that the work consists of counting parking tickets. Humiliated, and refusing this, Yusef becomes that characteristic figure, a waiter: the immigrant as polite, uniformed and deferential servant, in a white shirt and bow tie, a napkin over his arm. Here again he is mistreated.

If I mentioned Kafka before, it was a little off the mark. The masochistic revelling and desire for humiliation is more like Dostoevsky, of whom my father was particularly fond. The first time I read 'An Indian Adolescence' I was struck by the mother's 'yellow parasol' as she stands at the back of the auction room. It made me recall the fact that my dad spoke on several occasions of the prostitute's yellow parasol in *Crime and Punishment*, as though the prostitute and mother had become the same person in his mind. But it was *The Brothers Karamazov* he was haunted by. My grandfather died in the mid-60s, one freezing winter, in the common ward of a Birmingham Hospital, where one of his daughters, married to a doctor, was working. My father, I recalled, talked of the decline of a once-great but extreme and eccentric Dostoevskian family, now scattered, humbled and divided. This was the story he wanted to write, when he had the time, and I think 'An Indian Adolescence' could have served as the first part.

Reading this book makes me think of what 'redundancy' means. I am almost fifty myself and think often of what I want to do now. Clearly, the questions posed by the second half of a life are not the same as those posed by the first. Most of one's work is done; the major decisions have been made. One feels jaded and played-out, as well as fulfilled in certain ways, and wanting new projects and pleasures. No one should want, at fifty, that which they wanted at thirty. What does one really want to do?

To have such a thought is a luxury. In contrast to my father, I find it almost impossible to understand what it would be like to lack the ideas and hopes I believe will give me pleasure, that keep the future alive for me. Also, I have never known, or had reason to fear, the humiliation of being unable to support one's family, that most basic, potent requirement of a father.

Throughout his life dad seems to have been preoccupied with the question: how do you find something to do which carries its own meaning, that is significant in itself, and which cannot be doubted as a value? This question also becomes, how should I live? Well, father thought that being a writer was the cure for doubt. Self-expression as an artist was the most important thing and its own justification. Writers are beholden to no one else, they are their own masters, and being dependent – on his brothers, for instance, or mother – made dad crazy.

If the absence of belonging is considered to be the immigrant's particular bugbear, dad was fascinated by another kind of belonging, which might be called a vocation. In this notion of my father's, there were two sorts of people – those who knew what they wanted to do, and those who didn't. My father was the latter but he wanted to be the former. The vocationalists were artists, politicians, scientists, doctors, devoted parents, anyone who was fortunate enough to be 'called' to a fulfilling task. Those who had something definite to do every day would be cured of internal disarray.

From my father's point of view, absolute fidelity to one idea was, paradoxically, more liberating than the anxiety of those who woke up wondering what they fancied doing. Those in this latter group, wavering and flitting, suffered from less meaning. They might easily become the slaves of those who did know what they should be doing. If my father had felt 'useless' for a long time, the answer was to create a purpose, like having an internal parent, giving commands. It would be an organising principle, a system of rules and taboos which provided a necessary structure. I suppose life can seem impersonal in large families; children can feel there aren't enough parental wishes directed personally at them. They can easily get lost, neglected, forgotten.

However, many of the writers I admired as a young man – Henry Miller, say, or Kerouac, or even De Quincey, and music heroes like Charlie Parker or sportsmen like George Best – seemed to represent a kind of desirable anarchy. They were artists who took their work and their pleasure so seriously that some of them were killed by it. This was something of a paradox for father. He wanted to be an artist and, later, he wanted this for me. But he didn't want anything uncontrolled to occur: mad words in a room rather than a mad life. The need for free expression wasn't supplementing a revolution; it was instead of it.

Therefore, although dad was the boss in our house, where he had made his own empire, there was another boss, beyond us, which created our existence. This was 'the office', a place where no one really wants to be. Who would go there if they weren't paid? Work – which Nietzsche calls 'the best policeman, it keeps everyone in bounds' – was the source of dad's income, even as it took most of his time and energy. Dad, like most dads, was either preparing to go to work or recovering from work. I don't think I ever knew exactly what he did in his office, but this ignorance gave his work an air of mysterious importance. The daily details, the tedium and futility, as well as the important contact with other Pakistani men ('I didn't want to work with foreigners'), I had little idea of.

Whatever went on in the office, I was certainly led to believe that it was more important than child-rearing or mothering, or having sex, or watching TV. It was this system of authority which determined father's state of mind – the state within which we lived – and which, as Colonel Murad had done, kept father in the humiliated state he wrestled with all his life.

If writing can be a record of wishes and reparations, then the character of Yusef in 'A Redundant Man', having given up being a waiter, becomes – rather too quickly to be believable – a successful corner-shop businessman, fulfilling the traditional dream of the immigrant. He says, 'My new Mercedes Benz had just arrived.' Yusef wears 'Italian leather crocodile' shoes. Dad doesn't fill in the details of Yusef's rise, it happens like magic; yet this imaginative account reflects a sort of social reality. For me it was bizarre, when I did eventually go to Pakistan, not only not to find the 'Eastern spirituality' I'd hoped for, but to learn that my family were obsessed with cars, video recorders and stereo systems; they were not really different from us at all.

It had been too competitive at home in India for dad, and he had been repeatedly humiliated. He was no admirer of Thatcher, who, like others on the right, fetishised competitiveness. There's no doubt that competitiveness, which cannot be without an aggressive or even brutal aspect, seems a peculiar quality to prefer above most others. It has its attractions, particularly in sportspeople or seducers, but not in teachers, say, or nurses, or bus drivers, where a Darwinian contest might be less relevant. Thatcher seemed to think that competitiveness and intelligence were linked, but why should they be?

However, hard work and competitiveness do usually accompany one another and I have written in my fiction about the immigrant as successful businessman, but there are earlier accounts. A writer who occasionally reminds me of Patrick Hamilton, Alexander Baron, has a scene in *The Lowlife*, written in the early 60s, featuring for the first time in British fiction – as far as I know – Pakistanis in the East End. The protagonist, a Jewish gambler and masochistic intellectual who has been told, by 'a tart', to invest in property, goes to look at a house. The owner has a shop.

> A Pakistani family lived inside. Judging from what I could hear, there was also a fair boatload of Pakistanis living in the upstairs rooms. Behind the counter was a little chip of an Indian in a powder-blue suit.

Inside the shop the hero gambles with the Pakistani owner and, of course, loses the house as well as his money.

As father was aware, if the colonising British in India were one sort of problem, the English in England were another, an unforeseen one from the immigrant's point of view. J. G. Farrell had written, 'The loss of the British Empire is the only interesting thing that happened in my adult life.' Colin MacInnes in his collection *England, Half English*, with its drawing by Peter Blake on the cover, called the 1950s 'an astonishing decade' because of what he describes as 'its own sharp imperial decline'. Discussing Shelagh Delaney's ground-breaking *A Taste of Honey*, MacInnes writes, 'What have we learned, elsewhere, about working-class child-mothers, ageing semi-professional whores, the authentic agonies of homosexual love, and the new race of English-born coloured boys? Or, to consider other contemporary themes, what really revealing things have we had about the millions of teenagers, about the Teds, or about the multitudinous Commonwealth minorities in our midst – the Cypriots, the Maltese, and the many thousand Pakistanis . . . and the vast pop culture?'

This was a hint at what was to come. Following on from the postwar proletarianisation of culture – the French and Italian cinema, Brecht, the Royal Court, and its culmination in Pop – was the introduction of black and Asian figures into the scene. Meanwhile, the British knew they had lost their central place in the world, and this wound made them dangerous, susceptible to despair and hate. As Alexander Baron implies, aimless and disoriented in the ruins of their Empire, the deposed rulers felt they might be robbed of what remained, perhaps by those they once ruled.

'The British were married to India,' wrote Enoch Powell, the only child of school teachers from Birmingham. His parents were used to being in charge, but they were not part of the ruling class. He himself was hard-working, inhibited and loved authority, as long as it favoured him. He was an old-fashioned imperialist at the wrong time. As Omar has described, like many Westerners in the colonies, Powell felt powerful and liberated in India. He learned Urdu, had two intense homo-erotic relationships, and soaked up India 'like a sponge', adding, 'I fell head over heels in love with India. If I'd gone there a hundred years earlier, I'd have left my bones there.' There is a lot of this in Forster, of course, and in Ackerley, who would not be the first to renew their art and life by contact with the 'primitive' that their sophistication kept them from at home. But there is irony and self-knowledge in their work, the full comic play of human character.

By the mid-60s, when it was clear that these 'occupations' could not be sustained in the same way, and Britain was in the midst of a different kind of self-reinvention, called 'the Sixties', Powell said, 'It is like watching a nation busily engaged in heaping up its own funeral pyre.' He wrote, 'Soon the black man will have the whip-hand over the white man.' He also spoke of the English beginning to feel they are 'a persecuted minority'. There will be 'domination' over the rest of the population.

If Powell claims to be afraid of the immigrant, dad's book 'The Redundant Man' is full of fear, too. Whenever Yusef leaves the house he is afraid of being abused or attacked. This paranoia does not seem to be exaggerated. After all, the part of Kent in which we lived had been the site of the Battle of Britain, and there were numerous bomb-sites in which we children played; in the garden of our house there was an air-raid shelter, filled with jam-jars, which became my den. Every local had its veterans at the bar; all familes had their own memories of both wars. Not that the war was much discussed at school, except in the most patriotic terms. If everything was the fault of Hitler, and had been mended by the hero Churchill, what was there left to say?

The fact that the Empire and the civilisation of Europe had cracked up and descended for years into barbarism and extreme violence posed the inevitable question: where does this come from? Why did millions of ordinary people – the sort who lived in our street, us, even – commit the worst imaginable crimes? The next question would have to be: when would it be back? The fact that one race had attempted, literally, to physically exterminate another, was a shocking truth, almost unbelievable in terms of the other things we like to believe about ourselves: that we had achieved a certain level of civilisation and control, that 'we', the British, were superior, for instance, to the 'natives' of India, a position preferable to the terrors of equality.

Who knows what the answers to such problems could be, but the questions weren't put. In school we were aware when a topic of discussion was 'alive'; we knew when learning was being used as a soporific. We knew the word 'irrelevant' and used it all the time.

And so, with the Holocaust in living memory – the man who cut my hair once showed me the number tattooed on his arm – a new form of racism emerged, this time directed against those in the former Empire, as though people couldn't live without racism, they really needed to express their hate in this form. It is important not to forget the racial and political atmosphere of the late 70s and 80s. There was the casual racism of graffiti and everyday contempt; the National Front was active, particularly in the East End and South London. In 1967, the National Front condoned Powell: 'What Mr Powell has said does not vary in any way from our view.'

According to the historian Peter Fryer, between 1976 and 1981 thirty-one black people were murdered by racists. There were violent marches in Lewisham, a couple of miles from where we lived, and later in Southall, where the demonstrator Blair Peach was killed. Among the most significant oppositions to this was Rock against Racism – the disaffected and liberal young, those whom Islam could only reject.

I was good friends with a local Sikh boy, and we both had English girlfriends. His parents worked and we'd hang out at his house all day, playing Screaming Lord Sutch and Deep Purple, having sex with the girls and messing about. He had a car, and we kept off the streets where possible because it was dangerous. One time we were chased by the local bad boys, but escaped because we knew our way around. The next day I heard that an Asian kid, mistaken for me, had been picked up by the boys and beaten so badly he'd ended up in hospital.

My father had been bullied and suffered racism in India and in Britain. But it didn't make him a victim in his mind. He worked with Pakistanis and didn't endure the kind of persistent and degrading racism that some of us knew at school and on the street, the kind which made you lose faith in the rationality and justice of the British political system, which had both required immigrants and collaborated in their persecution. It seemed, at the time, that one would never recover from this disillusionment. I guess this was partly because the racism my cousins and I suffered occurred when we were young. Therefore we came to believe that exclusion and revilement was our permanent fate; nothing would change and no one would make a space for us.

On my way to the local Indian take-away I favour at the moment, I stop in the little park at the end of the road to talk to Abdullah, who is sitting under a tree, drinking beer. As a strict Muslim he feels guilty about this and sometimes lodges the beer bottle inside his coat sleeve, which makes him look as though he has a broken arm. His family, if they knew about his drinking, would cut him off completely. He likes to talk politics, this Somalian, and in the evenings his little flat is usually full of other Somalians and other Muslim Africans – Sudanese, Ethiopians – who remove their shoes and sit on the floor when they finish their shift at the local bus garage. On his TV he can get twelve Arab television stations. A prayer mat is next to his bed; he shows me his Koran and his Labour Party membership card, though since 'Labour starting bombing the Muslims' he has decided to leave the party.

In the take-away I talk to the Bengali manager as I wait for my food. The manager refers to 'the white man'; Abdullah has just been talking about 'the whites', and I realise that they know they live under a reconstituted colonialism; this is not only a matter of racism but a question about how people like them live in a world dominated by white political, social and cultural power. Both men are suspicious of the whites, whom they both loathe and have to keep in with, while being wary of the whites' hypocrisy and cunning. According to this picture, the white man possesses everything and will not part with it willingly; not only that, everything white is better than everything non-white. Just as in Ellison's *The Invisible Man*, the non-white seems to exist, can only exist, in the gaps in the white world.

My grandfather, Omar, my father and the others took this polarisation for granted, as both a political and psychological attitude. They were living in a state in which a white elite presided over the non-white masses, even in periods of so-called de-colonisation. Despite everything, this continues today; despite the obvious racism, poverty and inequality of the United States, for instance, the white man knows more, and his values are always better. Everything else, in the rest of the world, is a falling away and is 'backward' or 'undeveloped'. It might seem that this is not always the case in culture, where the opposite sometimes applies: non-whites are hip, they have the energy of the marginalised. But allowing non-whites to sing and dance isn't the same as ceding political power. The white man is in charge and imagines he always will be, even as he becomes more and more paranoid, like Enoch Powell.

Before radical Islam, one solution to the question of colonialism – how can I live in this society as a non-white? – was to become powerful, the opposite of a 'victim'. The character played by Saeed Jaffrey in *My Beautiful Laundrette* is similar to this, not parodying the whites but becoming as serious at business as they are, a greedy Thatcherite preferring money to people, owning the means of production. Not that this always works.

In 'The Redundant Man', as a result of his transformation from humble worker to wealthy businessman, Yusef is called, with some condescension by his leftie, hippy son, a 'grocer'. In the language of the time, he is condemned for his 'materialism'. In turn the son, the father feels, has become 'too English' – as though, being born and brought up in England, he could be anything else.

At another point Yusef says to his son: 'You were a great cricket fan. Aren't you interested in it any more?' The boy replies, 'Naw, man. It's one 'ell of a bore.' The father reflects: 'Somewhere I had mislaid not only his childhood, but his Pakistani upbringing.' Yet father had always refused to speak to us in Urdu, and when we attempted it ourselves, mocked our accents. He wouldn't teach us about Islam, which we came to regard as pointless superstition. Once I gave him a Smoky Bacon crisp; as he swallowed I informed him what it was, that the pig had entered his body. He rushed into the bathroom and emerged foaming at the mouth, having washed out his mouth with soap. Even this didn't make him more loquacious.

Yusef's wife Salma – I would say she is a mixture of Bibi and my mother – is very religious. Often she finds her husband louche and repellent, and not without reason, in the light of how father presents him. She says he's full of 'devil-talk'. If Yusef is a self-portrait, it is a cruel and insensitive one, like someone bullying themselves. Father's self-attacks and, indeed, the Muslim part of him, partly find their voice through Salma. When she is there, Salma is vividly and insistently present, loathing and provoking the man; that is her place in the scheme of the book. Circling Yusef, all the characters are similar in that respect.

Having usually been in some sort of relationship with a woman, I can only be intrigued as to what these loves were like for dad. Yet there is really only one voice in 'The Redundant Man', and, in the end, we don't hear enough from Salma, as we don't hear enough from the women in the book I am now writing. Salma's 'foreignness' in England is not explored, though immigration is often more isolating for women than it is for men. It cannot be surprising that questions about immigration and the immigrant inevitably end up as questions not only about who we are, but who we want to be – the deepest things.

During several long conversations with her husband, we learn that what Salma wants is to 'save' her husband from his lusts by returning him to Islam. But, having been a good Muslim all her life, and finding her devotion unrewarded, by the end of the book she herself begins to lose her faith, something my father must have wished his own mother would do, to make more room for other things – him, for instance. For Salma, this anxiety about her faith might also be a 'worry' about the 'right and wrong' which my cousin's diplomat friend wanted; a worry about the idea that if you behave well, if you are obedient, you will be fulfilled. Yet my father as a writer is able to see that it is only when people realise that following the moral rules cannot be enough that their lives start to become more interesting, if not dangerous, to themselves. This is what happens to Yusef, and it is lively, though painful.

The protagonist has, once more, slept with a 'tart' – a woman he meets at a party at a friend's house. Her vulgarity excites him a lot. 'Sin is beautiful,' she informs him. In both of dad's novels, the best sex is either casual or paid for; and it is always taking him downwards, socially if not emotionally.

My father writes of his encounter with the woman: 'I had had a wonderful time. I had thrown off the shackles which Pakistani society had imposed on me. I felt liberated. I was back again, pulsating with life.' But his sexuality cannot go unpunished; it is designed to attack the family. For dad sexual pleasure and the family are incompatible. The family – good at least for the upbringing of children – is where sex stops. If the price of his pleasure is too high, what will he do? What will happen to that desire?

The next day, while suffering from a severe hangover, Yusef is visited by the local Moulvi who tells him, 'You're enjoying yourself drinking and womanising. And I hear you've started to neglect your family as well.' The Moulvi then attacks the miscreant with a Dantesque confidence few Western priests or vicars could manage. He reminds him of the 'scorching fires' of Hell, where sinners 'will scream with terrible pain', adding that Allah constructed Europe 'with all its easy sex and drink, to test the will of the Muslims, whether they remained steadfast to their beliefs or succumbed to the temptations'.

If my father was a foreigner in Britain, this book represents how strange he feels to himself. He is so incapable of comprehending what is occurring in his chaotic mind that he is almost delirious. The Moulvi attempts a 'cure' by reintegrating him into his world, by making him part of the community again, as if Yusef's problem was that he'd become too individual, too focused on himself. To rejoin the group, the brotherhood, the family, is to forget difficult bits of yourself. This is a remedy – of sorts.

But it doesn't work. I want to see it like this. What the Moulvi cannot do is translate Yusef's suffering into terms which are helpful to him, which illuminate his condition. Using the language of religion, the Moulvi can only tell him how to behave in the future, without giving him any insight into his present state of mind, its origins, its provenance, its nature. If disobedience and therefore separation is Yusef's curse, the Moulvi can only threaten and punish him, like Colonel Murad, so that Yusef feels guilty, angry and despondent.

Yusef cannot go home – where would that be? – and he cannot find a satisfactory emotional and economic position in England. He is offered nothing between materialism or belief. Nothing like culture, for instance, or ambition, or writing. My father hardly bothers to fill out Yusef's story; there is something more urgent he has to get down, about the feeling of redundancy, and of 'uselessness'. It is as disturbing as watching a parent have a breakdown.

As the book continues, the members of Yusef's own family seem foreign to him. Rereading, it dawns on me that I am a character in this story, the son. Here I am, according to dad or, rather, Yusef: 'I looked in disgust at his unshaven face, his grubby black sweater, greasy jeans and crushed white shirt.' The son he has created is 'a brown cockney bum'.

It is disconcerting to find yourself turning up in someone else's book, and I am not a pretty sight, dripping with CND badges and chains. The son is frequently doing things like this: 'He ran his fingers through his long black hair, which was tied at the back with a pink ribbon.' Certainly father and I had many conflicts at this time, and it is informative, to say the least, to hear it from his point of view. He hated my hair, my independence, my aggression towards him, just as I loathed his advice and his desire to humiliate me. Dad was a difficult man to disagree with; divergence seemed catastrophic, as though you were letting him down by having other views. At times I'd be speechless with rage, restraining myself from yelling back at him, fearful my words would do him in. I learned to control my furies, keeping them for the page. I was cool but the writing was hot. Eventually, I more or less shut up altogether, saving myself for writing, ruining my social life.

But not entirely, according to dad. There is a delicious moment in 'The Redundant Man' when the father enters the boy's bedroom to find a naked English girl lying on the bed, 'reading *Private Eye*'. In this scenario father himself is, of course, a kind of private eye. I like to imagine him listening at my bedroom door, going in when I was out, opening drawers, reading notes and diaries, generally snooping, as I did in my parents' bedroom. The boy claims, plausibly enough, that he is 'drawing' the girl. The father, with some kindness, blames 'England'. I can only be surprised at dad's fantasy of life in my bedroom, for in my diary of the time, aged twenty, I wrote, 'Couldn't make love to J yesterday, knowing dad was downstairs. Anyway my potency is going.'

Not that dad wasn't right to blame England. There was, at

this time, feminism and the drawing together of the sexes, leaving each to wonder who they were. The girl in question, imagined naked by dad, had lived with me in Morecambe. One time, when we'd returned to London, she came over for lunch and we were sitting in the front room when father came in. He took a volume of Chekhov plays from the bookcase and began to talk. 'Chekhov had a horrible father and numerous greedy brothers and relatives, blood-suckers all basically . . . But he managed to pull himself out of it by writing . . . This is beautiful literature.' Father, asserting himself, made it clear that no girl could come between him and his son. It wouldn't be long, then, before I'd leave.

That girl was to become a short-haired lesbian, a road-sweeper in Brixton, a teacher of girls in a Muslim country. My next girlfriend was to go to Greenham Common; she became involved in the miners' strike and the struggle for women's rights; later she went into local politics. Although men disliked what they saw as the 'stridency' of women in those years, the way men were objectified at times, they also envied the urgency of women's reading, talking, self-discovery and political purpose. They were in the middle of the revolution we all wanted, that we'd already missed out on once, in 1968.

In the early 80s the Greenham Common girl and others of our friends tried to drive the moribund Labour Party as far left as it would go, particularly when the middle ground was ceded to the newly formed Social Democrats. We sat through tedious meetings in grim halls on housing estates, the local kids throwing stones at the building while we voted on motions and 'composites'. We were young university radicals – gays, blacks, women – who had become lawyers, housing and social workers, getting into positions of power and taking over the Party, which wasn't difficult. In the workers' party, the working class were replaced by the middle class, and the old by the young.

And so, dad, it wasn't only hair and badges. For me, practical left-wing politics was the struggle with an unanswerable dilemma: how to reconcile the desire for equality with the cost of forcibly imposing it? It was clear, too, that any form of imaginative activity, or just having a free mind, was incompatible with the straitjacket of politics. I wasn't a natural father or rule-maker; I preferred to be the rebellious son. I could also see how absurd the socialist talk of comradeship and brotherhood was. Clearly there was no rivalry more poisonous than that of siblings, even if they were only pseudo-siblings, as in a political party. Furthermore, as a first-born son I wanted to be adored by my parents more than my sister; as an Asian who had suffered discrimination, I believed in equality. For me, the only place these puzzles could sit together was in fiction.

Mother was a different generation from the women I knew, striking out for freedom. Yet mother had once had other boyfriends and had lived in other places. There was a whisper of this in the present, but this voice became almost silent in the maelstrom of family life. Mother didn't enjoy the domestic sphere but hadn't been able to find another way for her desire, either through adultery or work. Father knew how he liked his women and he didn't favour them getting away from him. If he had been bullied by his brothers, he didn't want the sisters trampling on him too.

My father's two novels contain sexual relationships which have considerable impact on the protagonists' lives, yet this sex is split off: the sex in the novel is never with the woman he's really thinking about. He uses sex to get away from that, like a drug almost. Dad went to some trouble to avoid discussing sex with me. If, mainly to provoke him, I suggested we have 'a little chat about the facts of life', he'd flee, ordering me to do my homework. He would never ordinarily do that; I'm not sure he realised I had homework. Of course no parent, whether they talk about storks or about penises and vaginas, can explain the dirty reality of sexual desire to a child; it is always the erotic wildness which is left out, the point is always missed.

Another time: I was a pubertal schoolboy when the older sister of a schoolfriend tried to seduce me. In the holidays I'd go to their house. Although the parents were at work, we kids were supposed to listen to the classical station, Radio Three, all day. To escape this racket, we'd go into the garden, where the girl asked me to join her in a tent, suggesting I do whatever I wanted, to her. I was so excited I could only refuse. This was almost the first female desire I'd encountered. Terrified and fascinated, at dinner that night I told my parents. Mother was sympathetic, but father put his head back and laughed, seemingly delighted by the fact I wasn't up to it.

Dad liked my girlfriends to listen to him rather than be with me. He'd sit them down in the little front room and ask them about their lives, supplying solutions to their dilemmas. However, he did consider the white girls to be slutty, though he'd married a white girl himself. Later, he told me he didn't like my girlfriends staying overnight, in case the neighbours thought he was having them. Father disliked Muslim conservatism, but didn't like my sister looking 'tarty'.

If the immigrant always lives in a world he cannot quite grasp, he might seek to petrify it by controlling his children and, particularly, their sexuality. Can a parent choose their child's sexual partner and, if they do, what are the consequences? There is some of this in *The Buddha of Suburbia*, where part of the plot concerns a narrative dad and I talked about; together and separately we worked on various versions of it – the story of Jamila, whose father goes on hunger strike to compel her to marry. Even if she does comply, as Jamila does, the child inevitably turns into someone the parent cannot quite recognise, someone who can never be enough like him, because she was born later and in another place. And then the child leaves, as does the girl at the end of *The Buddha* and the boy at the end of 'The Redundant Man'. These separations are unbearable to the father, perhaps because he believes he has caused them. He certainly can't control them. It wasn't until I had children myself that I could see how parents might hate or be made depressed by their kids growing up and then leaving; that the particular pleasures of adult and child will be over for good and a quite different, and even more difficult, kind of relationship will have to take their place.

The play, 'Grocer and Son', which dad seems to have written around the same time as 'The Redundant Man', is basically the same story but with a violent twist. The father is as dissipated, the son as wayward and 'on drugs'. My father disliked self-indulgence, or, from another point of view, pleasure. He left that to his father and brothers. He was keen on self-control, for which he used yogic concentration techniques; he went to work regularly, whatever the weather, inside or out; and he was keen on controlling others, filling them with his wishes and instructions. The anarchy is in the work, where artists often prefer to keep it, living bourgeois lives. In 'Grocer and Son' the son steals from the father, robbing the shop till, for which the father beats him up. The son flees the family, which devastates them. Without the boy there is no purpose.

'The Redundant Man' was, I think, rewritten in the mid-80s, when Thatcher believed that acquisitiveness and materialism would take care of people's needs. It seems, to a certain extent, that father is ironising the immigrant here. Yusef has succeeded in Britain, but he has lost his wife to religion, and his children to England, to the culture he did, and did not, want to join. The immigrant parent is amazed by how much effect the environment – Britain – has on the child he and his wife have made. Then he becomes wealthy in order to avoid the special position the immigrant holds in the heart of the host community: to be loathed for his strangeness, helplessness and dependency. He avoids this fate, he escapes their contempt, but falls into terminal self-contempt.

I have to say that by the end, having read it twice this time, I was furious with my father and never wanted to see his book again. The arguments between Yusef and Salma over Islam, to which dad returns at the end of the book, seem interminable and go nowhere. Apart from the obvious fact that Salma and Yusef will be tormenting one another throughout eternity, the hopelessness of religion when it comes to dealing with internal conflicts, and father's inability to move beyond this, frayed my nerves. It also surprised me. After all, this account of the uses of Islam in the West was written before the fatwah against Rushdie, and before Islam as a political force became part of the West's consciousness.

Neither my father nor uncle, nor any of the other brothers, as far as I could see, were religious, yet this book is soaked in religious guilt and fear, and the terror of pleasure and lack of control. The dislike of alcohol, or any kind of physical life – including contempt for the only woman in the book who wants to please him – soon becomes a strain to read. Guilt about the money Yusef has earned torments him. What Yusef and his wife want, as my father did, is to be good children and seem innocent. Yet when innocence brings them nothing, they cannot understand why Allah has let them down. At least my father was able to see, because of his mother, that excessive devotion to religion is a form of narcissism, a barrier, in fact, between oneself and the world, a convenient way of neglecting the individual and replacing him with God.

CHAPTER NINE

'An Indian Adolescence' and 'The Redundant Man', written at different times by the same man, present quite different versions of the family. I'd always felt, by way of literature – and, later, films like Bergman's *Fanny and Alexander* – that the extended bourgeois family, Indian or not, was the real thing. Disaffected servants, numerous children, property and land, warring parents, authoritarian father, religious codes, murderous siblings, adulteries, betrayals and neglect comprised the late-nineteenth-century ideal. The version we lived in the suburbs, with its whiff of futility and loss, was a severely contracted idea of the original family – as the idea of the family itself mutated through generations, ending up, today, with single parents, with older people alone, in 'homes' which are not really homes. The suburban version was, of course, financially and emotionally more manageable for a father living in another country.

Yet it wasn't enough. Father seems to want to attempt, in the 'tart' scene in his book, to work out the relation between the family and the sexual pleasure of the individuals within it. Yusef wants forms of pleasure which will liberate him from the shackles of tradition, and from the self-punishing, mundane reality of work and family life. However, the form of the family is a given, and not modifiable, and the morally bad has to be defined as that which attacks it.

One of the shocks I felt, years later, when I split up with the mother of my twins, was due to the fact I believed that I would live my parents' life. Very little would change, as any disruption would be too painfully destructive to bear. However I'd lived until then, I saw a permanent marriage as the destination. I would reproduce my father's life: although extreme in its feeling at times – I can remember father becoming so frustrated he hacked at a mole on his face with a razor blade, until it bled – its structure never altered. Apart from the children leaving home, there would be no upheavals. But the suburban ideal only worked if nobody wanted too much, or if their wants were only material. The moment anybody wanted anything new, or wanted anyone else, the whole thing became a problem, and the price of satisfaction would be high, emotionally.

Suburban regularity was sustained by keeping disruptive people out, so the house became a refuge. In Karachi, however, the Kureishis began their Friday Nights, which sound similar to the 'talking parties' I went to in the early 80s, a mixture of political seminar and drinking session. In the 50s these were attended by journalists and British and American businessmen, as well as actors, actresses and luminaries like Arnold Toynbee, John Arlott and Zulfikar Bhutto. The third volume of Omar's autobiography is partly a hymn to male friendship, to those he had maintained good contact with for most of his life.

In our suburban version the numbers were kept down. Few people came to the house. Father knew the men he worked with, many of them recent immigrants. He'd tell me their stories. Mother had her family and a few acquaintences. It felt as if the house had become a wall, hostile to outsiders. Dad had always talked of 'irrelevant' people, of those who wasted your time. What was time for, then? When, much later, I began to write *The Buddha of Suburbia*, I saw early on that it couldn't be a simple autobiography; I had to open the family to influence and change in order to make the story dramatic and unpredictable.

I wrote earlier about finding good teachers, those who can understand what you want to do, and can extend it. It seems anomalous now, the emphasis on book learning, since a good deal of what I learned as a young man was from others, from conversation, being turned on by people and following their enthusiasm. The constant talk, in the suburbs, about the 'standard of living' had made me think of who your friends were and what they talked about. The 'standard of living' wasn't, in fact, just furniture, carpets, gardens. It was the atmosphere in which you lived.

Aged fourteen, having read a few long books, I decided to write one myself. The idea was to see whether I had the stamina for such a task. I had become drawn to rash challenges, provided they were sanctioned by dad. My father must have recognised that I was having trouble at school, that I was in danger of disappearing into despair and failure. Writing was his thing, the desire he lived with, but by introducing me to it, by showing me the satisfaction possible in developing a craft, he lifted my spirits and showed me a way out. As a younger child I'd wanted to be a painter, but as mother couldn't bring herself to continue, this wasn't something we could do together.

Luckily, I no longer shared a bedroom with my sister: my maternal grandparents had found their own flat. At last I had a desk, record player, radio and a heavy old typewriter father had somehow managed to carry home from the Embassy. So I spooled the paper into the typewriter and began. My diary says:

'The novel is the sad story of a Jamaican in this country, his two loves and racial problem. It is written in a modern, flowing style, appealing to all. I've tried to put the colour problem in perspective.' I wrote it after school, during the holidays and at weekends.

When the novel, 'Run Hard Black Man', was finished, I didn't show it to my father. I had offered him other pieces of my writing, but his criticism was surprisingly brusque and discouraging. From this point of view, no one was allowed to learn – you had already failed. It was the sort of double-bind which parents often present their children with: the child must follow the parent's project but should neither succeed nor fail at it. What possible solution could there be but to go it alone?

Fortunately, Omar was acquainted with a woman at a publishing house, Anthony Blond, whom I knew as Genet's British publisher. Blond himself invited dad and me to his office in Doughty Street, where Dickens had lived. I was wearing my school uniform; dad took a day off work and urged me to ask them for a £5 advance so we could afford a good lunch. Dad always believed that the highest form of critical appreciation was cash. Blond, I think, wanted to see whether I was really the age I claimed to be. Fortunately, he wasn't intending to publish my book, but thought I should continue to work on it. In the office he introduced me to Jeremy Trafford, an upper-class editor, in charge of the academic list. Trafford had been brought up in India and had worked in Pakistan. He had also been a hippy, and, along with being well read, was an aspiring novelist. He lived in shabby, traffic-choked Earls Court – bedsit-land, full of Australians, tourists, whores, dealers, alert-eyed fags and chancers. It had its own dirty beauty; I was to find that the only uninteresting parts of London were the wealthy areas, like Belgravia.

Jeremy loaned me records and books, and guided me in my reading. At Jeremy's parties, enthusiastically attended by queens and young men, as well as eccentrics and female novelists like Beryl Bainbridge, and at which people sang Noël Coward songs, declaimed poetry and behaved as they wished, I was shown off. My father, as Jeremy puts it, was 'puffed-up with pride'. I was amazed, in comparison with the lower middle class of the suburbs, by how many words and how much information the metropolitan crowd had at their disposal. So this was what education was for – better conversation over food and wine.

On Sundays Jeremy would come to the family house and sit with me at my desk, going through the sentences in my manuscript, striking some out, complimenting others, talking about the words and images that worked and the ones that didn't. (Nietzsche calls the creation of all art a matter of 'rejecting, sifting, reforming, arranging'.) Jeremy would also write me long letters about the nature of fiction, and what made it most effective, about creating structure and, most importantly, character. He believed writing could be taught, and this laid the basis for my actual writing. He showed me how to revise and develop my work, and became furious when I did it too quickly. I got the idea that writing wasn't something that one did alone. Real others, and the critical others one had in one's head, were essential. His close attention and encouragement was an important outside validation, demonstrating that my writing wasn't only narcissistic but had some value in the world. I wasn't writing for my own benefit alone; I had to make something that others might want. This was a turning point.

Over all this my father was patient, but excluded. Such praise and attention wasn't something he had received himself. To receive praise is to compete with others who also want it, and that could raise a sibling firestorm.

I had begun to take my work seriously, partly because Jeremy had done so, and because it had occurred to me that unless I had a project, my daily life could turn into a repetition of my father's. Apart from writing, I had no other talents. Most of the professions I would have liked to have considered – architecture, psychoanalysis, academia, film directing – I hardly knew existed. The view from the suburbs was that, as the world was terrifying, one should keep as far away from it as possible, hugging the known.

This early foray into the book world separated me from my former friends and made me consider school, and everyone there, a waste of time. But one day a boy from school, not a kid I knew well, invited me to his house for the evening. I supposed we'd watch TV and gossip about the teachers. Instead, in his bedroom, I found him dancing on the bed, wildly playing the violin, an instrument he had clearly never picked up before, accompanying a record by the Velvet Underground. He was wearing his school blazer, except it had been slashed into strips. The walls of his room were what any mother would call 'a mess'; he had decorated them by throwing pots of paint at them. Sitting around, cross-legged on the floor, were boys from other schools, including Bill Broad – later to become Billy Idol – who was at the Grammar School and wore little round Lennon specs and a duffel coat; he had an American accent too. To my surprise several girls were already there. All evening and into the night people came and went, with albums under their arms, some of them playing guitar together, 'jamming'; or they commandeered the bed and copulated with the girls. I stayed until it was light, and went back the next day.

These kids called themselves 'freaks', which was how I saw myself. They didn't, though, only want to watch Disney's *Fantasia* on acid in Bromley Odeon and mess around at festivals, waiting for Soft Machine and the Maharishi Orchestra to come on, but were thinking about what they would do in music, fashion, photography. They made me feel competitive, so that before getting into my velvet trousers, I'd do a couple of hours at the typewiter, trying to see what sort of stories I could make out of our lives, stories I hadn't seen in other people's books: teenage sex, overdoses, sadistic teachers, the weird lives of parents when perceived by children. Chekhov was a great writer, but there is always something shocking and exhilarating about seeing the contemporary world in fiction.

Dad went to work in pink or purple shirts, his cuff-links dazzling; his ties were often psychedelic, his shoes had 'snazzy' little chains or buckles attached to them, his socks were bright. Dad taped music for me, sharing his enthusiasm: he liked the blues, soul, gospel, reggae, and anything on Tamla Motown. Omar grew his hair longer too, and wore more informal clothes. Throughout the 1960s, in Pakistan, Omar worked as a journalist and continued on the radio. When the Pakistan team toured England he would be on Radio Three, as well as writing for the *Guardian*. At family gatherings and lunches, depending on which uncle and combination of cousins was present, we would cluster round the transistor radio; or we would see, if we were on the beach, others listening to him.

A Pakistan cricket tour of England was a time when I could see the brothers together. Talking in a mixture of Urdu and English, the brothers would gather to watch cricket; Test matches, of course, lasted five days, of which they wouldn't miss a minute. They would smoke, drink beer, bet, tell stories and jokes, rib one another, and argue and dispute ferociously. I would see how rough this could get, how hard the brothers might be on one another. It would be puzzling, but something of an illumination, that the most difficult relationships one could have would be with those one knew, and liked, best.

Omar often passed through London, usually in connection with cricket. For a while he was manager of the Pakistan team. I saw him most consistently in the early 70s, around the time East Pakistan broke away from West Pakistan to become Bangladesh, and the consequent invasion by India. It was in 1971 that Zulfikar Bhutto became President of Pakistan.

Omar had a small service apartment just up from Battersea Bridge, opposite the Roebuck Pub in the King's Road, Chelsea. In his black polo necks, he smoked his cigarettes the way I had seen Ken Tynan do on television. Various women would come and go, and they'd talk to me and ruffle my hair; I can remember a girl taking off her thigh-length boots in front of the fire. It's an image I've never forgotten, and it's something I wanted for myself, over and over. I remember, to my mother's disgust, Omar taking a group of friends out to dinner and the bill came to £100. 'How can he spend so much on food?' she said.

Once we arrived to find Omar turning on the radio to catch up with the news when George Harrison's song 'Bangladesh' came on. Being enthusiastic about the Beatles, I urged him to let me listen to it, but he snapped it off and turned away. I could hardly comprehend what this simple tune meant for him and for the other brothers; in other words, the disintegration of what they considered to be their homeland, a place secure from both colonialists and Hindus. In *Home to Pakistan* Omar says that the East Bengalis were being treated as natives, 'much in the way the British had treated their subjects'. There wasn't even a common language. West Pakistanis spoke Urdu and those from the East spoke Bengali. Keeping the two 'wings' together had been almost impossible, and the conflict made Omar wonder whether any part of Pakistan would survive. Living in Britain, I had no idea what it might be like to wonder about the viability, the very existence, of one's country.

When the brothers' political discussions became too much, or when Omar went into another room to talk on the phone to his and my father's schoolfriend Bhutto – 'Good morning Prime Minister,' he would say – I would leave the flat and walk up and down the King's Road, looking at the shops and people. The only other place like it was Carnaby Street, in London's West End, which I had visited with schoolfriends. I came to dislike returning to the suburbs. It was tiring and boring, the late-night train to the suburbs, followed by the wait for the bus and a long walk, as well as being too reminiscent of my father's journeys on the train.

It was occurring to me that I could leave, indeed, that I would have to leave home and the suburbs in order to have more of these city pleasures. But I was afraid. What was the relation between pleasure and safety? What did your pleasure do to others? Wasn't that called ruthlessness? How did you survive without your parents? My father had always had a steady job. My uncle Omar didn't; his carelessness seemed to bring him more good things than others' caution. I'd have to learn how to write, but how did you do that? Could you make a living at it? I'd stare at Omar as he talked, wondering.

Writing this, I can recall being struck by something James Baldwin wrote. On his first day in church he was asked, 'And whose little boy are you?' What could he possibly answer, except 'Yours'?

I know I've got myself muddled up. In many fairy tales and religious parables there is the real family and there is the imagined one, as in love there are real people and the phantoms we mix with them. The way these realms mingle and merge is the stuff of fiction. I thought I was one thing but really I'm another. I can see that now. Mother didn't like Colonel Kureishi, who tried to force her into the kitchen to cook for him. She'd been an adored child; unlike the other local children who were 'evacuees', she'd stayed at home during the war, her mother refusing to part from her. She wasn't keen on any of the Kureishi brothers, apart from father, whom she idealised. She didn't understand my liking for them, representing it as a betrayal. I guess father had unloaded his resentments onto her. Naturally, this made these men more intriguing to me. I saw, early on, how essential it was for me to resist mother's disapproval and incomprehension of alien life-styles, but it led to a necessary split between us.

It must have been difficult for my father to see me fascinated by a man he was so rivalrous with. Or perhaps he wanted me to see what he saw, to see that which hypnotised and petrified him. But if my father was devastated by the fact that Muni was going to be married to someone else, and that his mother preferred God to him and that he had to share his parents with numerous other siblings, he would have been aware that there are unexpected and painful forms of infidelity ahead – for example, a son with his uncle, your own brother – which can be even more complicated.

CHAPTER TEN

I left, or, rather, was ejected from school at sixteen, with no educational plan. It was made clear that the kids who were hippies, mods, skinheads or rockers were not required in the Sixth Form. Anyway, I had only three O-levels. The teachers had no ambition or hope for themselves, and certainly none for us. Perhaps a handful of us would go to university; the rest would leave school at sixteen and become apprentices, work in insurance or go to technical college to learn a trade. For a lot of kids, Pop was the only hope for a creative, unpredictable life. The mother of a schoolfriend gave her son, for his birthday, with a mixture of belief and despair, a guitar and amp, telling him to 'get on with it'. Otherwise we were locked into the postwar vision of a controlled – married, of course – and secure life, the life my parents wanted to live.

One of Jeremy's acquaintences might have suggested I go to Fleet Street and become a journalist, but I knew already that that wasn't the sort of writing I wanted to do. This is partly what it means to be lower middle class: unless your parents have more expansive ideas, the notion of who you can be is severely limited. It is the Other who is qualified to receive the good things. Class isn't only a matter of ambition or accent: accents are variable and easily changed or learned. The working and lower middle class didn't speak as much. Being articulate wasn't a virtue; it was regarded with suspicion. You were too

The author, 1970

self-conscious, snobbish even. The male movie stars we idolised were still mostly silent.

I became aware of the significance of these distinctions later, particularly at the Royal Court, where most of the older directors came from military backgrounds, and had been to public school and Oxbridge. The most radical among them still had the accents of colonels, though they attempted to identify with the proletariat. Their confidence, narcissism and sense of what they were owed were staggering. Of course, my father came from a public school and military background; his father had been a colonel and the family had a strong sense of entitlement. Not unlike the boy in *My Beautiful Laundrette*, my job was to restore the family fortunes, to return them to their rightful position. But how?

I'd always had a paper round; I liked getting up early, when you could feel the quality of the air. Dad would be up and dressed already, writing at his desk in his suit before he left for work. I'd walk the deserted streets with my dog, even if I'd been up late the previous night. Not far from the house was an art college whose newspapers I'd deliver. At 7.30 in the morning I'd wander the deserted corridors, go into the classrooms, sit at the desks, open the cupboards, and read the notices for political meetings, bands, and 'happenings'. I'd write anonymous stories and poems on pieces of paper and pin them to notice boards around the college. Walking home for breakfast, I'd count the condoms in the bushes.

One day in the summer, realising I had no idea what I'd been doing that autumn, I went to the college and made an appointment to see the English lecturer. My father didn't know how the English educational system worked, and my mother was withdrawn; all she'd said was that she wanted me to join the Navy. She could see that one of us needed to get away, but it was the late 60s and I had no love for that kind of authority, having already been in the Air Cadets where, learning the cornet, I had been much fondled by men in uniform. Fortunately, the art-college English lecturer, who must have been in his mid-twenties but wore a cravat, seemed to believe that if someone wanted education they should be given it. There was a far less structured approach to exams and qualifications than there is now, and I was let in.

The art college was more like a university than a school. I preferred being a student to being a pupil; students still had cachet, they were making the revolution, and colleges were as much playgrounds as institutions. The lecturers and students were indistinguishable and they were, naturally enough, sexually involved. Yet information was exchanged and enthusiasm encouraged. If it was a relief to be there – if I felt my life would always, now, be different – it was because the chances of being spat on, abused and beaten up for being a 'Paki' were far less than they had been at school, where I'd been locked in a room in the woodwork shop and attacked with chisels, and burned in the metalwork shop. Had I stayed on I might have been destroyed by racism. Despite this, my first college girlfriend wouldn't introduce me to her parents since she knew they'd go berserk if they discovered she was going out with an Asian. But I'd been to her house, and the back garden was next to a bus stop where I'd stand, looking through the fence, watching her and the family. There will be much of this corner-of-the-eye stuff in any childhood, the kid's attempt to watch a drama through a keyhole, witnessing only fragments and filling them in imaginatively while feeling excluded.

At college the smell of dope was ubiquitous; bands came down from London to play, and poets like Brian Patten and Roger McGough gave readings. You could even get to see *A Clockwork Orange* at the Astoria in Bromley High Street, or go up to the ICA to see Godard films. (The Sex Pistols played at the college in 1976, where they met my friends in 'the Bromley contingent', spawning other punk and new wave bands like Siouxsie and the Banshees and Generation X.) I spent so much time in the students' union, where people lay around on cushions listening to music, wearing fur coats from Oxfam, talking to an array of people I'd never have met at school, that I was made the student president.

The lecturers took us to the theatre, and it was at college that I read Genet, Plath, Hughes, Larkin, Thom Gunn, Eliot for the first time. It was, too, the first time I'd been in a class with girls since primary school. These young women – who took LSD and used heroin, had affairs with the lecturers, and discussed contraception and abortions – liked to tease me about my paper round by asking what was in the papers that day.

I may have been bookish, shy and naive, but as a boy I could recall dad looking at women, the shame and curiosity as his eager eyes took them in, brightening when they came close: he led me to them in ways he can't have intended. But where did looking take you? The world may have been full of such opportunities but he appeared to have no more use for women than looking; or it was better to keep clear of the whole thing. His was a theoretical enthusiasm, which mine couldn't be.

At college, where I should have been happy, and was happy, I learned how easy it was to fall in love, discovered how many attractive people there were littered around the place, and how compelling it was to get your hands on them. I experienced the essential wretchedness of love for the first couple of times, racing rapidly through the whole cycle: illusionment, bliss, doubt, jealousy, boredom, stasis, disillusionment, hatred, mourning, renewal. There I learned that once you have entered this cycle it is impossible to halt at any one stage, or to doubt that the whole thing, which will be repeated, is a form of madness; what goes on in your mind and body is not something you can will. You might wonder what it might be like to enter this repetition in something like full knowledge of what Philip Roth calls 'the facts' – perhaps found in books or gleaned from friends – as though this might make a difference, when, in reality, it cannot, and should not.

This enchantment is described by my father, focused around Muni, in the middle of 'An Indian Adolescence' and is completed in 'The Redundant Man', where he explores the bitter futility of the exhausted marriage of Yusef and Salma, who are unable and unwilling to satisfy one another, and are incapable of separating. As full of advice as my father usually was, this was an area he shied away from – the central experience of a person's life: what it might be like to try to sustain an intimate relationship for years, while remaining alive. Perhaps father hoped there was a way of avoiding such disappointment, maybe by being a writer, or by taking books as a substitute, making a zone where such searing conflicts didn't take place, as though literature – either making or imbibing it – created a saving distance.

What I also learned in these early relationships was that love and sex, taking you out of your family, led you into the strange field of other families, from which vantage point you could see your own family as an objective item, as just another struggling family in the world, as opposed to it being the entire world, and that this was disconcerting, like questioning a religion while wanting to believe in God.

CHAPTER ELEVEN

In my late teens I'd pick up whatever books were lying around the house. This was a good way to learn, randomness being a virtue. I'd talk with dad about his reading, too. I also read Jack London, Henry Miller, Jack Kerouac, Charles Bukowski. These were 'books for boys' or even for 'wild' boys, which countered the suburban ideal with a more spontaneous life. In my diary I called them 'life-style' novels and wrote: 'I don't want to go to school. I shall become a social drop-out and travel around the road, writing and fucking.'

Turned on to the idea of some kind of 'beat' existence, I wanted, after taking my A-levels and living in Morecambe with a girl I'd met at the art college, to forsake education altogether. But dad, who had insufferably strong ideas about how people should live, rightly decided I had to be a bourgeois. After many arguments with my father, I got into King's College, London, to read philosophy. The college had turned me down twice, though I refused to accept it and, with father pushing me, returned to argue my case with them. Today I am amazed by the persistence and strength of will I had then, and can only regret my inability to exercise it in other areas.

At college I knew intuitively what I wanted to study. At King's Wittgenstein was the department's deity; he had taught many of the teachers and visiting professors. Wittgenstein was perfectly integrated into British life – he didn't write about pleasure or sexuality but about language. Freud, whom I was ready for, was more awkward: luckily one of his sponsors was Richard Wollheim, whose lectures I attended and admired.

I began at last to find my way in education. Learning started to seem important when I figured there were things I needed to know in order to survive. I had recognised that the reading of fiction can increase the possibilities of consciousness, showing that there is more meaning and interest in the world than you might have thought. Reading a novel was like being with a fascinating person who was showing you their world. For me, philosophy was another kind of concentration. Theories seemed ways of creating more categories of apprehension. I found that it is not answers you find here, but better questions.

It had already occurred to me that that which made me who I was, was unavailable to my consciousness. I might be confused, restless and even unhappy, but I had no idea why. Although the idea of the unconscious was first formulated by Leibnitz in the early eighteenth century, philosophy, as Freud pointed out, had always been sceptical of the idea of the unconscious. To me there seemed no doubt that the deepest things in our lives were hidden. How did you get into the locked box of this inner world? Through myths, symbols, poetry? Certainly, no one could see themselves just by wanting to. I needed another angle, more tools, some other viewpoint. I needed to believe, too, that knowing certain things about the self was curative. Knowledge, as Plato liked to think, made people feel better. 'Who are we?' and, therefore, 'How should we live?' were philosophy's central questions. It was at the heart of all our lives, and culture was entirely concerned with it. So philosophy, like literature and psychoanalysis, seemed to be a particular kind of attention to what was going on and this attention was called, by both Plato and Freud, Eros.

Anyway, King's College and the King's Road were just along the District line from each other. The King's Road continued to be my playground, and the Royal Court Theatre was next to the tube. In my second year at King's, a short play of mine about students, 'Soaking the Heat', was discovered by dad on one of his forays into my bedroom and sent in to that theatre. In retrospect, dad seems almost more ambitious and confident on behalf of me than he was for himself. He knew, though, that I had been going to the theatre a lot; it seemed particularly lively at that time. I liked performers and audiences, any art which was enjoyed collectively. The play was given what was known as a Sunday-night production; it was rehearsed for a week with good actors on a minimal set.

It was the first time I'd heard actors speak my lines, or seen how a director shapes a piece of work with its author. I liked rewriting in the rehearsal room; it was where the jokes went in, and where I learned I wanted to write comedies. At the end of this single performance, which was by no means a triumph, my father was more furious than I'd seen him for a long time. He'd complained about getting all the way up to the top of the theatre, the number of stairs, and then about the size of the stage, which he considered too small. At the end I sat on stage taking questions from the audience. Whenever I looked up I could see dad was in rage: for a start, he was giving me contemptuous V-signs from his seat. I should have guessed that whatever happened the production would be too little or too much for him.

At the Royal Court and particularly at Riverside Studios – an arts centre in West London, where I worked later – I became interested not only in performance but in the actors, dancers and musicians themselves. As with travelling players or jazz improvisers, I liked to believe they led speculative and creative lives, far removed from the routines of suburbia. I was fascinated by the collaboration of audience and artist, their willingness to enjoy one another, and the depth of pleasure possible in live performance. I wanted to be close to that which was just being created. I saw, at Riverside, that an artist can renew himself through other art forms as much as through his own; that more abstract forms like music, the visual arts and dance can be as stimulating as words.

At times I still worked at the Royal Court, selling programmes, reading scripts and attending workshops. I usually preferred the intervals to the shows: working there as an usher I picked up more girls than I did later as writer-in-residence, and, when the show came down, you could have sex with them in the toilets. I caught glimpses of the great actors, writers and directors who were working there, Beckett, Lindsay Anderson, Bill Gaskill, and the younger generation, David Hare, Richard Eyre and Christopher Hampton, who introduced me to the famous agent Peggy Ramsay, who'd looked after Joe Orton. She represented me only briefly but seemed to believe, in her old age, according to Simon Callow's book about her, that I'd set fire to her office. In the early 80s I would see my name outside the Royal Court, when my play *Borderline*, about immigrants in Southhall, was performed in the main house.

Borderline was a 'group' piece, a play put together by me, the actors and director, based on collaborative research in an Asian part of London I was unfamiliar with. This way of working was difficult for me. I'd liked the isolation of writing, which seemed partly the point of it, and it reproduced, of course, father's lone-liness. But at the Royal Court working in groups was taken for granted. As Roger Michell pointed out to me recently, no soon-er had you come down from university to work at the Royal Court than you were on the train to the East End, where you were expected to run an acting workshop for forty socially deprived school kids, having never done such a thing before.

Long before grasping the fact that groups reproduced, in fan-tasy, the family dynamic, I found them difficult. I didn't much like to listen, particularly to anything I disagreed with. Listening to dad had at times made me frantic. I found it almost impossi-ble to speak: like some children, I chose to be silent at home, in order to reduce family conflicts. Therefore, in the group, I'd be in such a temper I could hardly stay in the room. I was remind-ed, too, of being at school; maybe I was reminded of how much I needed other people. Yet I stuck with it. A good deal of my work in theatre and film has been collaborative, and after being persuaded to run writing workshops at the Royal Court, I began to see what groups were good for, the kinds of intimacy and self-revelation possible when strangers started to meet to discuss their lives and read their work to one another. I came to see groups as a 'third' space, between being alone and losing oneself in a large organisation. The purpose – writing – was still personal, but you saw where others fitted in.

At the opposite end of the King's Road to the Royal Court was the flat where Omar had lived. In terms of who I knew, there were at least three aspects to the King's Road. Apart from the actors, writers and directors at the Court, further down there were the wealthy playboy types, the sort of males who would later be characterised as 'medallion' men. They were accompanied by posh girls, later known as Sloane Rangers, who mostly lived in Fulham and South Kensington. (These were the women Omar knew and, in class terms, I believed to be outside my range.) This group, which was also semi-gangster – though antiques rather than drugs were the currency then – drove expensive cars and hung out in the bars, and cafés like Picasso's.

On the other hand, because of the proximity of Malcolm McClaren and Vivienne Westwood's shop Sex, the first generation of punks drank in King's Road pubs like the Roebuck, the Water Rat and the Chelsea Drugstore. Upstairs at the Roebuck was particularly rough and I was shocked by the violence of the punks, particularly after being hit on the head with a beer glass. Some of the kids had come up from the suburbs like me; I'd been at school with them, and those who weren't in bands had begun to work in fashion and photography. The others included self-destructive council estate boys from places like Kilburn, and they weren't messing around.

It was during this period in London, the mid-70s, that I left home for good, going to live in West Kensington with my girl-friend, who was reading English at King's. I think my father was shocked by my leaving, by how sudden and definitive it was, that such a passionate involvement can just end. It seemed to make dad iller and more bitter, as though he wanted me to fail in London and be forced to return home where the two of us would continue as before. My father had left his parents' house in Bombay and never returned; my mother lived close to her parents and saw them every day. Which parent would I be? A mixture of both: I felt bad about leaving, as though I might suck all the life out of the family and should protect dad and mum by giving them something significant to do. Being concerned about the fate of dad's writing was how he got us to worry about him, how we all kept him hopeful. Nevertheless, if a parent's duties to the child are relatively clear, the child's to the parents are less so, particularly as the child gets older. What exactly do you owe to them now? Why are you being more loyal to your father than you are to yourself?

Two parts of the King's Road were represented by my closest friends at university, both Eastern European. Like *The Buddha of Suburbia*'s Karim Amir with Charlie Hero and Matthew Pyke, I'd always had a penchant for hero-worship. I was brought up on sport and, later, on pop, so that Lennon, Dylan, Jagger and Hendrix were my masculine ideals. After leaving home, my propensity to find fathers and brothers who had better lives than me – however fractured, self-contradictory, and dissipated they might be – seemed to increase. As my mental state frayed, the lives of these others seemed more glorious. However, if a life can be narrated in terms of identifications, it will have told be told in terms of those you leave as well as find.

Brian, a Czech, was born here; Georgi was Bulgarian. Neither of them had English as their first language. Brian knew London, its pubs, clubs and bars, far better than I did. Georgi escaped Bulgaria in difficult and traumatic circumstances and had applied for asylum. He was good-looking, had been an Olympic cyclist, and read Hegel in bed, in French, though it didn't appear to cheer him up. Both Brian and Georgi seemed to embody different aspects of Omar for me – his carelessness, intelligence and charm. Both were self-destructive in ways beyond me.

These two good friends of mine, both interested in philosophy, were never particularly interested in each other. And if friends are those who lead the lives you wished you could lead, they stood for different things. Most of the punks were working class, or pretended to be. Brian and I were not working class, but our backgrounds and that of Georgi were not easily located in the English class system. We were all, somehow, displaced, without being intimidated; we didn't believe there was anywhere we couldn't go. Down or up, it was the same, and the two met in rock'n'roll.

Brian was interested in the media and in sexual extremity. He had a magazine, a band and an older girlfriend. The day we met, he took me into a bookshop to show me the work of Allen Jones. We were both obsessed with the Rolling Stones, the Beatles and the Sex Pistols; sometimes we'd sit around whole evenings, often on LSD or having swallowed a chunk of dope, listening to music, talking about it.

He borrowed money with no intention of returning it, never kept appointments, wore your clothes, stole your booze, told lies, and would have sex with your girlfriend while your back was turned. With his own girlfriends he was sometimes violent, often abusive and always mortally dependent. He said he wanted to be loved as a man – unconditionally – not for his actions. I said actions were the man and not even babies were unconditionally adored. He introduced me to PVC raincoats, to the work of people like Gensis P. Orridge, to pornography, the idea of group sex and amyl nitrate, as well as to various clubs where transvestites, queens and artists hung out. We were always trying to get into Derek Jarman's parties, held in warehouses in the East End. In those days the various 'underground' groups were less clannish than they became, and tended to hang out in the same, mainly gay, clubs, like the Sombrero, in Kensington High Street, and the Blitz, just up the road from King's College, in Holborn. Brian's girlfriend began to work as a prostitute, mainly servicing Arabs. Punk – violent, ugly, self-destructive, anti-hippy – was the perfect cultural expression of young people who'd been abused as children.

I was with Brian on my twenty-first birthday, which occurred in my second year at King's. We were with the woman he'd introduced me to, who would become my girlfriend, and with whom, that night, I was having sex for the first time. We'd hung out most of the night smoking dope and listening to punk singles – 'God Save The Queen' had just been released. The next day when I phoned home, mum said dad had had a heart attack and was in hospital. I came to believe, of course, that there was a causal connection between the events – my absence, having sex – and father's illness. Anything my father didn't like was rebellion to me. However, I knew that wherever I went and whatever I did, he was, like God, always watching and condemning.

As far as I was concerned, Brian and Georgi had forceful desire for women. They were more committed to their pleasure than they were to their future. Like Omar, they were boastful and bullying, but their adventures seemed real enough. I liked to hear their stories, as I'd listened to my schoolfriends tell of their early sexual adventures. My sexuality was in listening – in plot, detail, atmosphere; I was far more fearful of my impulses than my friends were. I went for straighter, quieter girls and felt I was conventional in comparison to my friends.

One night I discovered the price Briain paid for keeping his charm and activity going. He started to buy heroin, take a little himself, and sell the rest on. Suddenly, everything he had wanted, along with his talent, glamour, intelligence, charm, became reduced to this. The hippest thing was self-destruction. Boys who wanted to survive were weaker than those who didn't. If it is in the nature of mothers, and of the world, to be, ultimately, unreliable, there's nothing as reliable as an addiction. In comparison, I felt embarrassed about seeming greedy, asking so much of the world. Ambition was self-belief and hope. I wanted to be able to say, 'I write for a living.'

One of the ways I got to know London was by way of its pubs. In Bromley, my English grandfather had gone to the pub most lunchtimes, sitting in the public as opposed to the more salubrious saloon bar, reading the pink racing paper and the *Daily Express*. I liked to go with him. Soon I was going to some pub or other most nights, either in Bromley or in Beckenham. It was cheap and the only place for older teenagers to go. You met friends and strangers, read the paper, scored speed, marijuana and LSD, saw bands and even plays, heard music on the jukebox – it always seemed to be Bowie; it always seemed to be 'Suffragette City' – picked up girls, or at least looked at them, and escaped the parents. People talked in pubs, and there was no TV. So, living in West London and trying to write, at the end of the day I liked slipping into the darkness and the early-evening quiet of any pub where no one could disturb me. A drink would indicate the impossibility of doing any more work. Brian led us to the pubs by the river at Hammersmith, and there was Notting Hill which was bohemian rather than fashionable, before the pubs had been converted into bars. Some of this world, particularly the early days of dance music and the use of Ecstasy – a drug I liked too much – I described in *The Black Album*.

Brian, in particular, knew where to go. He and Georgi, who

worked as a croupier and sometimes as a bouncer, would go out separately every night, all night; they didn't get up until the afternoon. They seemed to go wherever they wanted, exploring the city, whereas I was locked up with my work, which they found risible and confusing. Brian had been mocked and beaten by his father; his curiosity and intelligence could barely survive his self-hatred, as he sat around for years in other people's flats, doing nothing except score and have his friends wonder what had happened to his promise.

After leaving university I did various jobs, mostly working in the theatre, either backstage or in the box-office. The major task of those years was to sit at my typewriter for days and days, weeks and weeks, in freezing rented flats, bored or with a hangover, in the attempt to discover whether I had stories to tell and characters to speak them. I got to my desk regularly and even stayed there all morning. I wrote plays and pornography, a novel, articles and my journal. The short story as a form suited me because it was easier to control; you could see the whole thing at once. But I liked bigger stories too, with numerous characters from different parts of society. It was editors, directors and friends who kept me going back to develop what I was doing. I began, also, to work on several projects at once, which slowed all of them down but made me feel busy. There was no way around it: I had to determine whether I could bear the commitment, patience and setbacks necessary for being a writer. And – as important – find out whether, unlike dad, I could locate an audience for my work.

You write, initially, out of preoccupation, expressing half-realised concerns and daily fears, which will have considerable emotional force behind them. They might seem like inspirations. It may be a while before you can see whether this material will be of lasting interest to you; whether you will want to live with it, developing it into a finished piece, or whether your enthusiasm will evaporate as the anxiety passes and other stories replace it.

I found I hated to wait, hated the frustration that any form of creativity relies on. To compound this, as you get safely further into a story and its possibilities multiply, the work becomes more absorbing as well as more fragmented and chaotic. You can feel schizoid, almost mentally unbalanced by what comes from this conjuring of inner spirits – the exaggerated love and hate, disgust, fury and perversion. It can feel like being unable to wake up from a nightmare. You hate the bad parts of your work; you hate the self who made them. How, then, do you make such material not only part of the work but part of yourself? Insofar as writing is painful, this is partly its source. The struggle to organise a rush of disparate and disturbing material can be disconcerting, which is why some writers like to work formulaically. That way nothing gets out of place and you can keep going.

But in anything genuinely creative there has to be a balance between the push to finish it, and the necessity of allowing it to evolve as far as it can go, for it to be as mad as it can be while remaining a communication. When I was actually working I found that I interrupted myself constantly. I'd get obsessive, frenzied and self-hating, hunting for useless stuff around the flat, until my head was in a turmoil, something I still experience.

Recently I wrote a short piece of text for the dancer and choreographer Akram Khan, and was made aware of the young age at which Indian artists start, and of the uses and constraints of the discipline and submission tyro performers are inducted into. There is a proliferation of fathers, gurus and authority figures in this tradition. Individuality and rebellion are not considered to be virtues. For these performers, the discipline isn't an extra, it's a way of life. This is one picture of the teaching relationship, which begins with the initiate's faith in the magician/authority, and has to end with the authority being transcended. If the artist can be inspired rather than crushed – if they can learn to use tradition rather than being intimidated by it – it will provide a depth of culture and ability which will inform and extend their work. Of course, in the end, discipline can only take you so far; it might get you to your desk, but when you're there your Eros has to be engaged, otherwise the work will be dead.

As far as I know, writers are the only artists who don't have a tradition of being taught. Through their reading, education and conversation writers have to create their own canon and purpose. What, then, might a teacher do? I have noticed that young writers often have the idea that the free production of their own images and feelings will damage others, that their creativity is a fateful form of aggression which others – mainly the parents – cannot survive. A teacher might have to show them that survival is probable, that there is a strong and useful connection between aggression and creativity.

As well as this, writers have to find good readers, friends who can grasp what they're trying to do. This is essential because often, if you tell someone that you are intending to become an artist, you will receive a painful and complex response. The other person, too, wants to be an artist. They are about to begin, but haven't got round to it. And, surely, you never seemed like an artist to them. Just how talented do you believe yourself to be? Do you really believe that others are that interested in you?

Father must have had to put up with a lot of this. He lacked support and attempted to find it in me, his prop, confidant, brother. However, in my view other writers aren't best suited to this job. Yet encouragement is essential because of the ambivalence any artist will feel about the yoke of their work: the discipline, which can make you feel as though you are being compelled by an internal tyrant; the necessary refusal of other distractions; the feeling of being trapped in your art, of having focused everything in this while others are really living, the hatred of having to start writing, stop writing, begin again, the whole damned cycle.

One thing you do need in order to write is to have others around you who are writing too, writing books you admire. The American formalism and experimentalism of the 1970s, which were, along with the French *nouveau roman*, based around the use of language, were highly regarded in some, particularly academic, quarters. It was of interest – language had been the preoccupation of the twentieth century's most important thinkers – but there was something dead, or too abstract, about it. No writer can afford to forget that a good story is always irresistible, that it is narrative rather than aesthetics which compel. Fortunately, from the point of view of my generation, Latin American literature turned up in Britain in the 1970s, reintroducing the human into the novel. Dad liked Gabriel Garcia Marquez, this man who wrote down his grandmother's stories, writing of places which were not America,

Paris or London. I liked Marquez's stories as well, and fancy they were the sort of thing dad might have done had he become the writer he wanted to be. Marquez was, of course, preoccupied with dictator-fathers, and no one looking at the twentieth century can avoid thinking of our love and need for dictators and their henchmen, torturers. Marquez seemed to be an author for a place like Pakistan, for instance, with its penchant for monsters, magic and extreme religion, able to capture figures as louche and divided as, for instance, dad's friend Zulfikar Bhutto, murdered by his successor Zia Al Haq, who was also murdered, a man fond of adjusting the constitution of Pakistan according to dreams he'd had the previous night.

I was moving out into the world and my education was just beginning. I was interested in the early Wittgenstein and his desire to separate what could be said from what couldn't. Wittgenstein made an analogy between philosophy and therapy; part of the point of both is to free oneself from illusion. Although Wittgenstein, whose sister was analysed by Freud, considered *The Interpretation of Dreams* to be Freud's most important work, he thought Freud was wrong about dreams. For him fears rather than wishes were the ultimate subject of a dream. It is probably too easy to reply that one's fears and one's wishes could turn out to be the same thing. When I left home, instead of plunging into the world as it seemed Omar had done, I found myself to be so full of terrors I could hardly go out.

I liked having a best friend – it took two to keep the world at the right distance – and Brian was almost the only person I could tolerate. As we were compelled to attend few lectures and seminars, Brian and I spent long afternoons strolling around

West London pubs and parks, talking about girls and philosophy, and sometimes discussing our dreams. He would say something like, How would your life be different if you started taking your dreams seriously? I wanted Wittgensteinian sense, and had tended to think of dreams being the preoccupation of soothsayers and fools, but was made to recognise that the idea of dreaming itself will certainly have a place in each family. We didn't, for instance, tell each other our dreams over breakfast. This said something, of course, about what is hidden. There is sexuality, but no dreaming, in dad's adolescent book.

When my uncle Achoo told me I wanted to have sex with my mother and kill my father – or was it the other way round? – I thought a great deal about such ideas of the hidden. Then I began to read philosophy which, as Freud acknowledges, has little time for the idea of the unconscious. I returned to Achoo, saying, 'I've never heard a convincing argument for the existence of the unconscious.' 'But you dream, don't you?' he replied. 'And, anyhow, what would a convincing argument for a poem, symbol or song be?'

At night, lying in bed, I began to imagine the sleepers in the city, lovers, prisoners, children, the dying – the nightworld as a factory of dreamers. I would think of the amount of symbolism and elusive desire pumping from their bodies, night after night, year after year. In a dream you are psychically naked. Yet how well-crafted, original and staggeringly apt these strange and often beautiful visions are, which can only be read by a clumsier, conscious mind. I became fascinated by dreams when I saw how useful they could be at the start of each day's work, as a way of beginning. By both describing and associating to them, I could write immediately without wondering what I had to say.

Brian and I would also tell one another our masturbation fantasies, as it was his practice to ask girls theirs. Certainly they're far less discussed than dreams. Such intense fantasies, conjured up as they are – cheerleaders for the final affect – appear to lie half-way between works of the imagination and dreams. But what do they say and do, apart from the obvious?

We were reading philosophy, studying logic and causality. But what was considered to be nonsense made another kind of sense too, and seemed to capture something: religious notions, emotion, wishes. I began to realise how little of our lives is spent in anything resembling a wished-for 'rational' state. There were dreams, daydreams, revenge and reparation fantasies, sexual and masturbation fantasies, imagination and creativity. One's investment in the world was via fantasy; fantasy and reality worked upon one another continuously, creating a symphony of mental phenomena which were not at all like trying to find an answer to philosophical problems.

I can see that as well as attempting to learn from books, I was trying to find out what was worth knowing. What sorts of knowledge are there, and what uses do they have? There was the book-learning of some of the brothers, as though they were preparing for the ultimate exam. There was my father's search for himself via Eastern esoterics; his desire to formulate values, a moral grid perhaps, a wisdom which would orientate you.

But there was another form of knowledge: Omar, Brian and Georgi's idea of sexual awareness, of the force of desire, which was more like a novelist's knowledge. It was a way of understanding the darkness of the other, of not only sexuality but of destructiveness, fury, passion and violence, of what other people wanted. This was a form of knowledge that brought you closer to yourself and to others, as well as to the idea of the writer as the investigator of the forbidden. And this was more like understanding dreams, or being interested in bodies – their signs, gestures and childhood subtext – and the crimes committed on them, than of liking books or wanting didactic information.

What do people think their preferred profession will do for them? At King's, where I had often found myself at a loss, I discovered that J. S. Mill was a good example of someone who thought they knew what their vocation was, but found that they really didn't know what they were doing. There are occasions when you feel so alienated and estranged from your own desire, that you lose the ability to live at all. 'Who', or where, are you living from? At times the 'foreigner' can only be grasped as a mad part of yourself. This confusion, Mill discovered, could be overwhelming. It could also be converted into experience, or literature.

Despite Nietszche's remark that the most significant philosophy was autobiographical, showing a subject's attempt to grasp something important for him, most of the philosophy I read turned out to bear no relation to how I felt. It emanated from minds rather than selves. For selves I would look to fiction, or to essayists like Montaigne or Camus. However, being told to read J. S Mill's *Autobiography*, I was struck forcibly by the chapter entitled 'A Crisis in My Mental History':

> I was in a dull state of nerves, such as everybody is occasionally liable to; unsusceptible to enjoyment or pleasurable excitement; one of those moods when what is pleasure at other times becomes insipid or indifferent; the state, I should think, in which converts to Methodism usually are, when smitten by their first 'conviction of sin'. In this frame of mind it occurred to me to put the question directly to myself: 'Suppose that all your objects in

life were realised; that all the changes in institutions and opinions were realised; that all the changes in institutions and opinions which you are looking forward to, could be completely effected at this very instant: would this be a great joy and happiness to you?' And an irrepressible self-consciousness distinctly answered, 'No!' At this my heart sank within me: the whole foundation on which my life was constructed fell down. All my happiness was to have been found in the continual pursuit of this end. The end had ceased to charm, and how could there ever again be any interest in the means? I seemed to have nothing left to live for.

Mill, clearly disintegrating, didn't know whose advice to seek. His father, whom he had successfully failed, was, as he put it, 'the last person to whom, in such a case as this, I looked for help'. Dead in feeling, he was isolated; even worse, he was unique, he had never met anyone who had felt this way.

Depressives like to believe, of course, that there are others who are not depressed, who have stable, inhabitable minds, normality becoming an ideal by which they punish themselves. Mill could only wonder how long this punishment might continue. The implication seemed to be that he would rather die than continue to suffer this inexplicable melancholy. Yet it changed his life, working as a form of rebellion leading to independence.

For Aristotle, melancholia wasn't a worthless state but was a form of thought, of painful philosophical enquiry. Mill never stopped reading, but turned from history and philosophy to poetry, art and music, which he called 'instruments of human culture'. He found relief in Wordsworth, Coleridge and Byron. He saw that culture was where painful states of mind were creatively lodged, and that there were others like him, who had written their suffering down to have it known by others. To his credit, one solution that Mill eschewed was that of turning his self-disgust into the hatred of others, a route Enoch Powell took, loathing the Indians he had once lived among and liked.

What appears to have brought J. S. Mill back to life is a death. It was registered in a passage in Marmontal's *Memoirs* 'which relates his father's death'. Moved to tears, Mill wrote: 'From this moment my burden grew lighter.' Though he could barely admit it, Mill took pleasure in the thought that the father's realm had been attacked. At the same time he knew that beyond the father's order there were no instructions. Leaving the father's house was to venture out alone.

My father had tried to give himself, and me, a vocation; he believed, as Mill's father did with education, that it would be sufficient for a life. The parent wants to give the child 'everything'. What else could anyone want? But there are states of mind, which I began to experience, which made me wonder if I were really the person my father thought I was and wanted me to be. Perhaps he'd got the two of us muddled up. I felt a similar liberation to Mill's when I opened Sartre's autobiography, *Words*, where I read the sacrilegious line, 'I loathe my childhood and all that remains of it . . .'

If I read my diaries of the time – the end of the 70s and throughout the 80s – there were occasions when my symptoms, phobias, fears and sense of futility incapacitated me. I was self-absorbed, but not really thinking about anything. My body felt heavy, but my words were light. They had no meaning, because meaning had been driven out. Conversation, silence, going out, staying in, awake or asleep, whatever I did, was blank. 'My nihilisms', I called it. Feeling wretched in this particular way – attacking yourself – takes all your time and energy. Such a condition is the opposite of what Nietszche calls an 'experimental life', or 'inner spaciousness'.

I liked women, their bodies and their concern for me. Sometimes they liked me. I had girlfriends, but there was always a moment when I had to flee them. The things I've wanted the most, I've fled. I liked to believe I was happiest alone. I even took drugs alone. Or I'd be stoned without telling anyone, but not so stoned that anyone would notice, living in a private state, my mind concealed. I was afraid of being overwhelmed by the other person, of there not being enough of me and too much of them; that they had more words than I did. Or that the differences between us, and the arguments they represented, would become unbearable. Or that I'd become so furious with them that I'd explode.

I became blocked as a writer but didn't know why. The words were jammed inside. I knew that they were in there somewhere, but some law I didn't understand was holding them back. The words, if released, would have catastrophic consequences. Something which should have been happening was not happening.

If I was afraid, during this period, of not having a 'voice' as a writer, this was not because I was unaware that I had one already, but that I was ashamed of it, of my desire, hatred, passion. Freud writes that often, when it comes to shame, it is not only one's masturbation one is ashamed of, but the fantasies – the aggressive imagined fulfilment of erotic wishes – which accompany it. Writing, amongst other things, is a form of extended fantasy; and since fantasy, daydreaming and the imagination are already linked, one cannot be surprised that there is inhibition.

It might seem strange, in this time of pharmaceutical intervention, that one should characterise depression in terms of language rather than brains, as though the melancholic is afraid of conversation. Yet talking is a free form, and words can take you anywhere. The melancholic will know this somewhere, which is why there will be sentences he cannot speak, and certain sentences he won't want to hear. Best keep away from all of it, pull the curtains and lock the doors.

I wrote: 'Laziness, inertia, failure. This breakdown has been going on for six months. The wheels in the mind are not connecting with the engine of action. Father says it's a middle-class illness, a form of uselessness.' A little later there is this: 'My father has told me he has six novels in mind to write. He's still at work, while I'm lying around in West Kensington, doing very little. I seem to get stuck in rooms; I cannot get out.'

Depression works as both a symptom and attempted solution. The deadness – self-hatred, despair, isolation – is a way of suppressing or rendering invisible the conflict. Depression is a kind of 'fixity' in the onrush of life, a way of finding a safe place, beyond the strife, which is always between desire and obedience. These two go together; they make one another possible. Yet the pain of living such a disharmony is so unbearable that the resolution can be an enervating illness.

Artists and therapists will want to find words for the conflict. However, father's approval of my words would make them difficult to produce. The words had stopped coming, and words without a catharsis make one feel heavy. Full of unused words, I became immovable. But I required words for my own benefit, because I wanted to write. This was a tangle. Maybe a way round it was to produce words he didn't like, that were my own words – specifically, words that seemed disruptive to me, but which were necessary.

Father told his story – wrote novels – but if there was no one to hear him what independent meaning did his stories have? Is this like talking to yourself? Family therapists and those who work with groups often use story-telling, speaking and listening in their work. The subjects get to put their point of view, to find their own words, to 'express' themselves. Speaking is preferable to silence, but words without a reply can feel futile. The writer speaking from himself in this mood is stuck. These are the only words he has, and they're not good enough: they're on a loop. The feelings he has are too powerful; the words he applies to them cannot dissipate them. What he needs is to have his words recognised in ways which seem liberating – liberating because they generate movement and new thoughts. This, of course, is only possible when your life begins to seem almost unbearably strange to yourself. Writing this, I am reminded of one of the most helpful and moving things said to me at school, by the woodwork teacher. When you came here, he said one day, unprompted, you seemed happy and full of life and enthusiasm. Now, five years later, you seem to be in despair.

I thought no one had noticed. Useful recognition, then, sees more than you can, enlarging the self; however, it can only come from elsewhere, and if there is no God how do you find it?

CHAPTER TWELVE

Philip Roth's novel *The Ghostwriter* is, among other things, a book about two writers. Having read one of the young protagonist's stories and been appalled, the boy's father takes him aside and says:

'This story isn't us, and what is worse, it isn't even you. You are a loving boy. I watched you like a hawk all day. I've watched you all your life. You are a good and kind and considerate young man. You are not somebody who writes this kind of story and then pretends it's the truth.'

'But I did write it. I am the kind of person who writes this kind of story!''

Roth, an American Jew whose grandparents were Hungarian immigrants, is a writer whose words were considered scandalous by his family, by his community and, sometimes, by women. It was my girlfriend, the woman I'd lived with in Morecambe, who introduced me to his work. She told me that she and a girlfriend, along with the college lecturer we had in common, met to enact sex scenes from *Portnoy's Complaint* involving a banana. There could be no higher compliment for a writer. I went to his books immediately.

The immigrant family and its desire for integration and respectability, the self-obsessed son with unruly desires and a taste for goy girls, were right up my street. The belief in education and learning, the family's desire for their sons to be doctors and even artists – anything but not a failure – along with the son

being amazed by the father's oddity, seemed immediately familiar to me. Here there was no forced good behaviour or 'passing'; the son would be who he was, and wanted to be, without
social inhibition. As far as I knew, there was nothing in British
writing as apt, funny and sweet at this.

Nevertheless, Roth's work, as he explained in *The
Ghostwriter* and various interviews, had caused devastation.
The immigrant family and community, brought low in the new
country by straitened circumstances, was then satirised and
degraded by the crazy wilful son who insisted, as an artist's
right, on exposing them. Like many artists, by both analysing
himself and becoming his community's conscience, Roth had
separated himself from the group who believed he was one of
them. This community, far too conservative and paranoid for its
own good, would catch up in time, indeed would become fashionable, exotic, hip. On this side of the Atlantic, that there
would be a British-Asian literature, and that Asianness would
come to permeate British life by way of its culture, as Jewishness
had permeated American, and that it would become chic and
then tired, making way for other ethnic groups, had never
seemed inevitable. But it happened relatively quickly.

By becoming a writer, Roth's conditional isolation enabled
him to join another group, that of argumentative artists. Jewish
alienation, he learned, could stand for a general alienation, particularly among the young. Racism, colonialism, immigration,
assimilation, exile, identity: as long as the reviled, the excluded
and marginalised didn't stop talking, they could find a place and
an audience – that chosen home my father knew was there but
could never reach. Roth also promoted artists whose speaking
was blocked, the heirs of Kafka – Eastern European writers like

Bruno Schulz, Borowski, Skvorecky and Kundera (whose remarks on remembering and forgetting seemed particularly pertinent), who had not previously been published in English. These were writers living under a system the brightest minds of my generation wanted to believe in, the only viable alternative to capitalism. These writers made us question ourselves politically, as well as reintroducing a literary weirdness and experiment into the Sunday-afternoon-in-the-rain realism we'd become used to.

When we were preparing *Sammy and Rosie Get Laid*, Stephen Frears and I would visit Claire Bloom, who was living with Roth in Fulham, not far from me. As Frears and I talked to Bloom, Roth sat across the room writing, correcting proofs. Whenever I visited he'd be working at his pad, looking up to talk, and working on. He said he was working on a memoir involving a provincial college he'd attended. Fiction no longer satisfied him, he said. At dinner he told stories about Capote and Arthur Miller, as well as about Singer, who, he said, was the only living American writer to have a street named after him.

I had published some fiction and done a little travel writing, encouraged by Bill Buford who was the editor of *Granta*. Being involved with *Granta* in the early days under Bill was, in its excitement, like being at the Royal Court, or Riverside, or at Channel Four at the beginning. Writers not only need other writers to work alongside, they need publishers, editors, booksellers and a culture to support them. There were dinners with Richard Ford and Raymond Carver, the writers who'd brought *Granta* to prominence. And there was Bill's enthusiasm. He'd ring up and suggest trips, to Kashmir, Butlins, Brighton, Bradford. When I'd written a draft, and the magazine was about to go to press, he'd turn up at my flat, with a box of pencils, a sharpener and a rubber, and rip through every line I'd written. Edmund White, who considered himself an aesthete and Proustian, said he didn't realise he was really an American dirty realist until he met Bill. However, when Bill had done his work and gone, and I was left wondering whether, in a perfect world, I'd rather he hadn't removed so much, I'd usually decide he was more or less right.

A story I'd written, 'The Buddha of Suburbia' – in effect the first chapter of what became the novel of the same name – was published in the *London Review of Books*. I showed the story to Roth, despite his complaining, as a lot of occasional writing teachers do, about having to read his students' work. He wrote me a letter praising the story. He suggested where I might publish others and added, significantly for me, 'If you don't mind my saying so, I have a feeling you can give us your world more powerfully in fiction than in films – there is a great deal to be said for the precision here, verbal precision, very different from pictorial precision, more lasting, to my mind, and peculiarly more precise.'

One day the director Peter Brook was at Riverside Studios, meeting actors for his planned production of *The Mahabharata*. He was asking me about India, where I'd been only once. Brook, known for his efforts to find that which is alive in theatre, had turned to Africa and India to see what they could teach him – something Western writers, visual artists and musicians like Miles Davis had been doing for a long time. There wasn't much I could tell Brook. I thought of dad reading Maugham and Shaw. Being brought up under the Raj, culture, for my father, was only British and, to a certain extent American – Hemingway and

Fitzgerald; and my head was a mishmash of British sit-coms, contemporary American literature and pop. This wasn't what he wanted; it was Hindu mythology and symbolism he was after. From this point of view I was a failed Indian, a fake even, wondering what I had to be for others, who were disturbed by who I wasn't. Karim Amir, the protagonist of *The Buddha of Suburbia*, also working in the theatre, similarly disappoints. He is either too odd, or not odd – exotic – enough. Brook was interested in the Asian as cultural figure while the real Asian immigrant had to forfeit cultural and sexual pleasure in order to become established in the new country. The idea was that his children, or grandchildren, would have pleasure – those who hadn't become fundamentalists in homage to their father's sacrificies.

Writing plays and films had given me confidence as a writer, confidence in my material, but it was work mediated through directors and actors. I'd never, as an adult, completed a novel. The success of *My Beautiful Laundrette* had shown me, and others, that such subjects were of interest to the public. Stephen Frears, the film's director, had helped me considerably as a writer by encouraging my sense of fun and scurrility. 'Make it dirty,' he'd say. He liked jokes and wanted to direct cheerful, lively films; having worked at the Royal Court under George Devine he also considered it part of his work to present hidden and ignored aspects of British life on film.

This attitude remained part of my work for a while and informed my first novel, *The Buddha of Suburbia*. This was an attempt to put all my experience into a book, to think of a young half-Indian man in relation to a particular white world. It was published in 1990 and sold well; it was translated into thirty languages and made into a TV series.

Dad said he liked *The Buddha* but didn't think it was as good as his stuff, which he considered 'deeper'. If he felt it was a disconcerting picture of himself, he didn't say anything. He had, as I know now, been working on portraits of his own father for years. Nevertheless, the success of *The Buddha* stimulated dad to write harder and push more to get his work published. If I could do it, so could he. I guess that's how 'An Indian Adolescence' ended up at my agent's.

But my father was still sick. He seemed to have been sitting in the house in his pyjamas for years. He died of a heart attack in November 1991. He lay on the bed in Brompton Hospital, his shirt off and his once magnificent body written on by illness, crisscrossed with stitched scars from his numerous operations, his breasts and stomach bulging and soft, the chest-hair white. His death was unexpected; we were always at the hospital with him; this was just another visit. But he was gone, and there I was, out on the street at five in the morning, gulping tranquillisers, without him forever, and mother saying, 'I just want him to come home.'

Even as he had lain in that familiar place, the hospital bed, thinking he would soon recover, he had been full of questions and projects and talk. He never stopped pestering me about what I was intending to do, as though without him I would die too. Sometimes he sat up, his cupped hands in his lap, Buddhist-style, as he attempted to practise his breathing exercises with an oxygen mask over his face.

That morning I walked home and went to bed and stayed there. I was then living alone, having recently broken up with my girlfriend. I had no children or reliable friends. I saw no one for four days. I had directed a film, *London Kills Me*, which was about to be released. It was about a bright but lost boy struggling to make a life.

Most communities have public and familial methods or rituals of mourning, which begin the process of detachment. But we had no such thing. We didn't even know if father had wanted a Muslim funeral or not. Looking at my diary for that period, it is mostly accounts of my drug and alcohol consumption: cocaine, amyl nitrate, Ecstasy, alcohol, grass, as though I were trying to kill something, or bring something in myself to life. I had a big flat on two floors, in Baron's Court, West London, overlooking Queen's Club tennis court. But I slept in the basement, one of those familiar London places where you can lie in bed and see the feet and legs of those passing by. In the morning I'd lie there thinking what I'd score that day, and from whom, as well as considering, once I was stoned, how I would get down again, get to sleep. Then the cycle would continue. It was a full-time job.

I came to believe that being stoned was the state of mind I preferred. I'd wake up and couldn't wait to be stoned again. The best way to survive – to be free of one's anxieties, fears, hatred – seemed to be to lose one's mind altogether. Released from the harsh command of father, from writing as solution, drugs enabled me to talk, in some broken form, to others. But the old solutions could not keep working. I'd be in local bars with black guys, white girls, and hip white boys in 'grey polo-necks, tortoiseshell-rimmed glasses, short well-cut hair' – a description followed by this giveaway, 'Felt much older than anyone there and wondered about my obsession with pop, youth, music.'

Like dad, I'd always been interested in meditation and had found it was a good way to begin writing in the morning.

'Sitting' was where you might hear yourself without censorship or interruption, where you could attend to your incessant internal 'free talking' until it went silent. This stream of associations and the demands embedded in them revealed the self to the self, bringing conflict into the realm of significant discourse. This knowledge would be curative. An insistent child, once heard and recognised, would no longer be frantic.

But suppose the speaking and listening selves are so self-destructive, or disconnected or disturbed, that this form of benign attention becomes impossible? After father's death I find in my journal such things as, 'violent fantasies; thoughts of suicide'; 'I have never loathed myself like this before'; 'On the edge mentally, thinking people have been sent in cars to kill me.'

If the mad are those no one wants to listen to or be with, what if one can't bear to be with oneself? It seems a dangerous situation. Meditation can't solve this, if all you hear is static, noise, chaos. Neither can books, for you either go mad or kill yourself, or retain sufficient sanity to call the doctor – call for another self to understand the self. My parents had presented the outside world as not welcoming, as dangerous. They wanted me at home with them, safe. But the old safe was no longer safe.

It wasn't long after father died that I started going to the mosque. (I look at my diary, which says, 'Drink and drugs all week, plus a visit to the mosque.') I had visited one in Pakistan as a tourist, but had refused to accompany my cousins on their Friday visits. Father had talked about the childhood monotony of having to learn the Koran by rote, and of being hit with sticks by the Moulvis.

I was surprised by my cousins' adherence to the faith; their parents were, it seemed to me, basically secularists. But I did, in

Karachi, have an odd conversation with Sattoo, when he asked me whether I was a Muslim. While making it clear that no one intelligent could swallow the superstition, and that no one wise could condone the moral attitudes, he seemed to believe in a basic adherence. When I said no, that it didn't make sense to me, he was surprised, or, rather, saddened, as though, foolishly, I'd excluded myself from something important, depositing myself in a kind of spiritual limbo. He lived in a world in which religion was taken for granted; you had to make an accommodation with it – to dismiss the whole thing was impossible.

I began to visit local mosques, writing:

The prayer area is in the basement of the large West London house. It is a long, low room – an extension – with ovals cut in the ceiling for light. Half of it is unfinished. There are appeals on the wall, including one which says, 'Claim your stake in heaven – give generously to the Mosque fund.' An American sitting next to me introduced himself and we sat and talked. He asked me if I was a Muslim, which I thought a bit odd, as we were in a mosque.

I was introduced to the Imam, who lives upstairs. He was a young friendly man, gentle, with a black beard, wearing a long green coat. He gave me a leaflet about Islam. While he was trying to talk to me an irate man came over and started arguing with the Imam about the mosque building work, saying why did you give it to a kaffir when you could have given it to me, who would have done it for Allah. Your estimate was too high, the Imam said.

I knew I had to remove my shoes, but otherwise had no idea what I was supposed to do there: dad had never shown me. I copied the others, finding I liked the men's faces: so many different races and types, together in the same place. It wasn't belief I was looking for: I already believed in culture and love as the only possible salvation, and Islam after the fatwah didn't seem compatible with any kind of combative imagination. I think I was looking for solidarity, to see whether there was a Muslim part of me that existed apart from my father, to see whether being part of this group could be significant, or therapeutic in any way.

I didn't find music, stories or community, as I had in church as a child. I found ideology and fundamentalism, and young people holding extreme, irrational and violent views, along with an inability to engage with or use the most basic forms of reasoning. It was puzzling: there was no attention to the inner life; it had been politicised. Behaviour, rather than thought, was all.

But I was curious as to why this was happening, and I went often, as well as to my local college where a Muslim group was based. It was disturbing to witness such hatred. Fantasies break, as they have to, on the rock of the objective world. But there was no semblence of the 'objective' world here; it was a hall of mirrors, and a cult of hate. I would hear the most rancid rants about women, gays, the West, liberalism, and soon got the impression that even the purveyors of such views didn't believe them, as though it were a form of satire and everyone already knew it was all vapour. This nihilism only contributed to the futility. I'd leave these people in a fury, feeling unclean, as though nothing had any value.

My father, whose own father was Westernised, often talked of feeling alienated in India with its numerous eccentric religions and superstitions. Achoo, too, had claimed that as an 'intellectual' he couldn't fit in. I couldn't lose myself here either; I didn't want to. But if I separated the ideology and the individuals, if I could get to the person behind the hate, I could find stories. I began to work on *The Black Album* and the film of *My Son the Fanatic.*

It was around this time – perhaps still on the look-out for fathers a year after dad's death – that I went to visit V. S. Naipaul in Salisbury. He had been among the first 'minority' writers to be recognised as significant; he had never been marginalised or patronised. Before 'world music', there were a few writers – Sartre, Marquez, Grass, Bellow, Atwood, Kundera, Gordimer, along with Naipaul – who were read everywhere and who transcended a particular national identity. I was anxious about seeing him. There was no Pop or bawdy in Naipaul's work; he lacked Roth's sexual fizzle and 60s attitude; he seemed depressed, an out-of-place immigrant wandering around the postwar city unable to find a door he had the nerve to walk through. He was disappointed by everything he saw, determinedly so. Soon it became an attitude. Oddly, in person, I found him to be friendly and attentive; like a lot of writers – like Chekhov, I imagine – he was more cheerful than his books.

After asking me whether I'd play tennis with him – I imagined that, like my dad, he'd give me a good beating – he told me he'd been writing that morning, but said he thought his best work was already done. 'It is there; it has been achieved.' However, as he liked to write, he carried on. I was interested in this because I was becoming aware that after a certain point much of your life exists in the past tense, and you begin to say, I have done this but not that. You are forced to lose hope in other possibilities.

Nevertheless, I did say to him that a writer couldn't know what his best work was, or whether any of his work would appeal to anyone. Perhaps this did not matter anyway. Naipaul added that it could take years for a book to reach someone who really understood it, but that time was not an issue. Books could hang around a long time, awaiting the right readers, or not.

I enjoyed my conversations with him, and wrote him long letters which were probably a little mad, about my father, his father, and writing. To his credit he didn't ignore me, but responded by ringing to talk about the novel as an essentially nineteenth-century form. This meant he was thinking of the best structure for his ideas, which he now called 'meditations'. He was looking for a new way of writing. It reminds me that, on the rare occasions when I take photographs, what pleases me is anything which contains a piece of the world in an original form, a form which is my particular way of seeing, but which surprises me. It also sounded as though Naipaul had lost his relish for creating character, and for story-telling, as though there were something louche about it, like an actor who believes that dressing up and pretending to be someone else is beneath him, and that there is something more earnestly worthwhile he should be doing.

During the writing of this book, I have missed writing fiction, the pleasurable freedom to be another, when anything can be said and done by the characters, uncircumscribed by some sort of fidelity to reality. I've missed the amusement and dream-like indulgence of pouring oneself into made-up figures, and the technical challenges of creating a story, of doing something so unnecessary and yet important.

Chekhov advised writers to keep a distance from their characters, to let them have as much independent life as possible without telling the reader what to make of them. For a writer it is freeing, and disturbing, to refuse omniscience, to let these characters talk. But to fantasise so freely can provoke shame in oneself; it can feel too pleasurable.

Chekhov's characters like to talk: it's all they do; they never stop telling us what they feel. His plays can appear to be like overlapping monologues. *The Three Sisters*, which Chekhov wrote in 1900, the year of the publication of *The Interpretation of Dreams*, begins with a father's death and two women talking about memory. The sisters themselves, educated, intensely frustrated siblings who wished to be elsewhere – preferably in the city – could have been among Freud's first patients. They seem to be paralysed, provoking Tolstoy to say to Chekhov, 'Where are you going with your heroines? From the couch where they lie to the closet at the back.' Tolstoy, like Chekhov, Ibsen and Wilde, put women at the centre of his work. And, as with Tolstoy, Chekhov saw that the frustration of these women's lives concealed something else. In an earlier story, 'The Duel', written in 1891, the young woman, Nadyezdha, is 'possessed by desire; breathing, looking, walking, she felt nothing but desire'.

Chekhov wanted to avoid the tyranny of deciding in advance the value of people's lives; judgement did not interest him – it brought conversation, and passion, to a halt. But a stream of self-revelation did interest him; Freud was similar. Chekhov's was a godless universe and there was, for him, no objective position and no one who could pronounce on its value or worth. This recalls Beckett, people talking endlessly and for nothing, because there is nothing better to be done. While Dostoevsky's characters were mad, Chekhov's were neurotic. His characters, not unlike my father, were looking for an ideal way to live, which they believed, when they found it, would render them happy at last. From a certain point of view their lives seem futile, but from another they're on the move, looking for better lives within a milieu that offered little to women.

Chekhov's stories are 'free form'. Few of them were written to a particular length or subject in order to satisfy the market. They emerged from inner necessity. For him, meaning and significance could be found in anything, in the everyday, rather than in the more notably dramatic. Chekhov liked to consider himself a comic writer, which is puzzling as his characters are always unhappy. It is not that they have 'problems' or 'issues' in our sense. This is the way they are – the only way they can ever be – and their despair is of the essence of life itself. Freud was more radical; he refused to accept this, having learned from his patients that certain forms of speaking changed people's lives. Freud wanted to reconnect people with forgotten passions, with their aliveness or Eros, enabling them to live better.

Philip Roth, in an essay written at the beginning of the 1960s, claimed that American reality was too much for any writer. Reality overwhelmed fiction, leaving nothing for the writer to say; it was always too little, too late compared to the contemporary grotesquerie. Clearly, looking at *Portnoy*, Roth's internal life overwhelmed him more than the world. Whatever was happening in America was irrelevant compared to his personal disarray. What he seems to be admitting is that you cannot write yourself out of such a state. Writing may be therapeutic: apparently Freud conducted his own analysis by writing rather than with another person. In *The Interpretation of Dreams* Freud tells us that he is able to adopt 'an attitude of uncritical self-examination . . . by writing ideas as they occur to me'. But for most of us, when it comes to self-examination, there is only so far you can go before you need to hear a voice from elsewhere. If there are omissions, significant unconscious metaphors and mistakes in speaking, who will hear them? Anyhow, why would Roth have to worry about capturing the American reality when it was in him already? Surely he knew he only had to speak and it would come out? He was the American reality.

My uncle Achoo had listened to mad children; he'd told me I had an 'unconscious'; sometimes he hypnotised me, and I remained interested in hypnosis, attending stage shows when I could, often attempting to hypnotise myself, counting backwards from a hundred and walking around the flat with my arms out in front of me. One day, convinced not only that I was going crazy, but that I would become insane within the next few hours, I visited a local hypnotist who worked from a council flat. He told me Freudian therapy took too long and often didn't work at all. Anyhow Freud was a cocaine addict who'd turned his daughter lesbian. The hypnotist said behaviour was a matter of patterns which could be rearranged. In the light of this, it seemed to me that the modesty of Freud's claims was a blessing. The hypnotist put me in a semi-trance but it did nothing for me except help me catch up on my sleep. What did interest me in all this, I realised, was the influence people had on one another – their mutual passion, as much the novelist's domain as that of the psychologist.

Just over a year after father died, I wrote in my diary, 'I have fantasies of being an orthodox, ordinary father in a suburban family' – though I was in no state for such a return. When I thought of having my own children I felt blocked; one father in the family had always seemed more than enough. Anyhow, while dad was still alive I was still partly a child. I went for psychoanalysis when I realised I couldn't see all of myself, read my own dreams, understand my own desire, no more than I could read my own work critically. My speaking, mostly to myself, seemed meaningless. For days – and insomniac nights – I would be lost in familiar and repetitive scenarios, confrontations with authority in which I would feel helpless, lost for words, unable to extricate myself, traumatic situations which must have already occurred, though I couldn't remember them. It was like someone playing loud music nearby, over which you have no control. In these situations you can only ask, who does your mind really belong to?

For Freud, psychoanalysis begins where hypnosis ends – or fails. I rang a friend who had started to see a young analyst. This friend and I had begun to meet for drinks at the end of his therapy. Suddenly there were long silences in the midst of our conversation, which annoyed me. I didn't like the idea of sitting in silence, it felt awkward, like being at home at the dinner table, where silence was a supplement to fury. But I came to consider the silence restful, like people meditating together. He gave me the telephone number of this man, who was the same age as me.

The analyst had begun to publish books. There was no intim-idating European austerity; he lived in the kind of disarray I recognised, books and CDs all over the floor, piled up and falling down. There was no waiting room; his patients would occasionally eye one another up in the café next door. I lay down on the wrecked sofa I would get to know well, a spring sticking in my back, the smell of the previous person's perfume on the cushions, and said, 'I feel aggressive and dead and frozen.' There was a silence. Something important had started.

(In *My Life as a Man*, Roth wrote: 'A silence ensued, long and opaquely eloquent enough to satisfy Anton Chekhov.')

Apart from *Portnoy's Complaint*, *The Catcher in the Rye* also used the novel as a confession to a therapist. I believed I could hear Roth's analyst Dr Spielvogel saying, 'Now vee may perhaps to begin. Yes?' *The Bell Jar*, *One Flew over the Cuckoo's Nest* and *A Fan's Notes* were all concerned with mental breakdown and the institutions devised to contain them. The monologue – free assocation's respectable form – which I used in *Intimacy*, had been a familiar model for me. The work of Bellow, Beckett, Kerouac, Ellison – writers far more macho and less interested in women than Chekhov, Freud and the others – was really nothing but this. These writers worked during a time of political commitment and turmoil, but the writer was very far from being able to see himself as part of a group, however sympathetic he might be to the working class.

I recalled Nietzsche's words: 'Every extension of knowledge arises from making conscious the unconscious.' Writers and psychoanalysts can be envious and rivalrous, both thinking they have the low-down on the human condition; both, of course, are concerned with tunnelling into the psychic interior using a similar device – words. Joyce sent his daughter to Jung; among other complaints she refused to speak. Joyce himself, who rarely stopped speaking, refused to be analysed by Jung and wrote, in *Finnegans Wake*, 'O, begor, I want no expert symaphy from yours brooms quadroons and I can psoakoonaloose myself any time I want (the fog follow you all!).'

The blank sheet of paper is like the analyst's silence, as provoking and as eventually revealing of the self's dimensions and desire. Some artists are afraid that by turning the light on an essential darkness, the analyst will steal their powers. Artists are not healthy; their art is the disease. However, you are as likely to lose your creativity through analysis as you are to lose your sexuality, or love for your children, by the same method. The fact is, many artists want to be cured of being artists, of the obsessionality which structures their creativity, an obsessionality which in its essence is as discomfiting as any other compulsion or addiction. Most artists work continuously, their production rarely ceases, and, if it does, this causes much anxiety and loss of meaning. The freedom to be an artist, rewarding though it is, is another form of bondage or slavery, as dad seemed to understand. If father's life and moods were determined by the train timetable, the life of any artist is controlled by as strict a timetable, internalised.

Freud called analysis an 'after-education', which makes it sound like a finishing school; but his method was also a merciless deconstruction of authority, of fathers, dictators, leaders and our need for them. Freud's friend and one of his first colleagues, Sandor Ferenczi, wrote about putting the analyst-father in the place of both the real and imaginary father. This would be a transitional phrase as you learn to live without the consolations and prohibitions of authority. In the end, looking at all possible cures, it is love that cures: love of knowledge, love for the group and group leader, and, in analysis, love for the analyst, who redirects you away from yourself into a new love for the world.

When my father was fifty, I was twenty and had left home. At fifty father was still trying to create the life he imagined was ahead of him, if he got the words in the right order. I'd like to talk to him about it, and have often tried to write a story about a man who goes into pub on his fiftieth birthday and runs into his father, who is also fifty. The two of them would have a conversation as equals for the first time, the son seeing the father as a man like him. The son would be gay, a theatrical producer, and the father going to meet a lover. I haven't been able to write a word of their dialogue; I can, though, see them walking away from one another at the end.

Just then I wanted to write: my memories of dad fade; they don't seem important; they haunt me less. But it's not true. I guess I dream of dad and other father-figures at least once a week, including last night, when the two of us were in the suburban family house, going through the cupboards. There he was, as a ghost, as tangible as ever. Yesterday, my son Carlo – in his woollen hat and football shirt, practising karate kicks or chatting about drumming – was talking about being an old man himself. As we discusssed it I knew, of course, that by then I will have been dead a long time, a ghost myself, undead to him, haunting him, and perhaps his children, in ways neither of us can anticipate.

Brian is fifty, and I am almost that age myself. We're still friends; he's one of the people I most like to be with, drifting around the city, drinking in the afternoons. In the old days the bars would be lined with bitter old buffers bemoaning the world. That's us now. I don't know what Brian's mental problems are, but years of alcohol and what he describes as 'the warm love' of heroin could only occlude them, so when he got dry and clean they returned, leaving him isolated, angry, unfulfilled, and much older. Oddly, I still envy him more than he envies me. He sees my books in a shop and says, 'You haven't wasted your time; a writer's life is a good one to have lived. Unlike me, you were lucky with your father, he believed in what you wanted.'

I adored his company, but it took me a while to learn I couldn't rely on him as a friend for support and understanding. One friend, however twin-like, could never be enough. I can see now that Brian reminds me of my father in his subversive charm, how he can say things you want to write down or think about later. But also in the way he conjures belief and hope in the other, on his behalf, which is then disappointed. What, ultimately, puzzles him, is the fact that, like my father, he has somehow contrived to live a worse, more frustrated life than his own father, despite having more opportunities. Brian's like someone who can't believe how things have turned out this way, as though it's all been a mistake.

Being fifty will be, I am convinced, the hardest birthday I have had, mostly because I have grown fonder of the world the longer I've been in it. There is still plenty I want to do but it doesn't seem a matter of survival, as it once did. As I watch my own sons growing up I like to think of my father and Omar together as children, playing sport, arguing over girls, talking

Author, Kier, Sachin, Carlo

about what they've read; and then with their lives lived out, one with his name on numerous published books, the other – dad – a relative failure in that respect, while his son writes this book, trying to bring everything together.

CHAPTER THIRTEEN

This project was supposed to end there: most of it written, some of it revised, and the final paragraphs more or less how I wanted them. It had been hard work, partly because the book began as an essay before becoming a kind of improvisation. I wanted to work on something else, a film I've had in mind, or the big novel I've been working on for years, for which I have hundreds of pages of notes. When I finish something my instinct isn't to rest, read, think, walk, but to rush into something else, to fill the space, keeping anxiety and futility – or some other unknown terror – away.

But before I could start again on the writing cycle, Monique and I thought we'd take Kier on a day-trip to Hastings, on the south coast, where Colonel Kureishi and some of his sons had lived.

It took us an exhausting four hours to get there. None of us fancied any more time in the car; we decided to stay the night and check into a hotel. This was more difficult than we'd imagined. We did at last find one with vacancies, and discovered that that evening there would be a parade along the seafront, followed by a bonfire on the beach and a firework display. The weather was good, the beach clean, the sea sparkling, the pier inviting. The hotel barman said they were having an Indian summer; not, he added, that Hastings doesn't have it's attractions all year round – the blind bowls championship, the bikers' meeting and the town criers' competition, for which people come from all over the country. I noticed from posters on the front that Elkie Brooks and Des O'Connor would be performing soon.

While we were waiting for the parade I went into a crowded pub on the seafront to watch the important England–Turkey match, a qualifier for the up-coming European championships. Beckham missed a penalty, falling over instead. The pub was rowdy, full of white lads in England shirts. They began to howl at the opposing players: 'I'd rather be a Paki than a Turk.'

The parade and fireworks were terrific. Next morning we drove back through Sussex and Kent, deciding to visit my mother. In the garden I said to mother how much bigger the garden looks now the flower beds have been dug up and covered with grass; she told me this was done in 1971. I showed Kier the air-raid shelter, which is still there.

I wanted to look at the family photographs again: Colonel Kureishi and my father outside Marine Court in St Leonards, near Hastings – Colonel Kureishi is wearing a suit and hat; I'd call it a gangster hat, very cool, and dad always liked outlaws and gunslingers, at least in films – and other photographs of my parents and myself on the beach in Hastings. Mother and I complained about one another to Monique, who soon became weary of our sniping and disputes. I asked mother again about the missing 80 pages of dad's novel. She shook her head and said, no, she knew nothing about those mysterious pages. She said she had found another book, which she'd been reading. 'The spelling is terrible,' she said. 'It is in the other room.'

It was a manuscript, but not like the others. For a start dad had both handwritten and typed this book on pages of A4 cut in half. I guess if the pages were smaller, there would be less retyping to do. The handwritten bits were scrawled on the back of old Christmas and get-well-soon cards, as well as on flyers for various spiritualist associations. This was really a hand-made book. Glancing through it, I noticed the names of the characters from 'An Indian Adolescence'. Mother said I could take it; in exchange, I said I would get one of her paintings framed. She repeated, as she always has: everywhere you look there are books – in houses, libraries, railway stations. Why can't one of them be dad's?

The manuscript was, it seemed, an early draft of 'An Indian Adolescence' containing material dad probably took out of the finished thing. In the car home I talked to Monique about what to do with it, complaining that I would have to go back into this book, now called *My Ear at His Heart*, integrating the new material. I went on and on about how tiresome it would be, just when I thought I had the book done. In the end she shut me up, saying: just read it, then make up your mind.

I got up early and begin to read. The book was untitled, and said on the first page, 'Not revised. Rough Draft.' Immediately the content seemed familiar. Shani and Mahmood were arguing over a bike Colonel Murad had bought for Mahmood. As before, the father favours Mahmood, forcing dad to wear his brother's old pyjamas. 'Mahmood was a pet of their parents.' When dad complains, his father slaps him, or beats him with his belt, neither of which he does in the version called 'An Indian Adolescence'.

It doesn't take me long to see that this is not an earlier draft or rewriting of the same book. For a start my father is younger: he is twelve and Mahmood is fifteen, and it is all set in Poona, before the move to Bombay, and written later, probably at the end of the 80s. For all of his life dad believed that the more you wrote the better you'd be at it; improvement was inevitable. This new work is certainly a superior book to the others, better organised, with some effective and lively scenes. All dad's books are basically free associations and set-pieces strung together. What dad can't do, or doesn't want to do, is create a narrative for each character. The people pop in and out as he wishes, without it occurring to him that the reader has become compelled by their story. This has to be the difference between someone writing for themselves and someone writing for others. This time, however, I think it will be less easy for me to patronise my father.

The maternal grandmother, Nani, is a significant character, more present this time. Dad doesn't know her age, but Nani's mother 'had been through the horrors of the First War of Independence in 1857'. He tells us, 'Nani was from Kashmir and had spent her youth in the rugged snow-capped mountains.' She would buy Shani a cycle if he wanted, but she and Colonel Murad don't get along.

Besides Nani, dad's other supporter in the house is Radna, the twelve-year-old daughter of a servant, who my father likes to play with. Dad goes to see her: 'Radna was sitting on a rush mat, outside a ramshackle wooden hut. She had spread before her a huge pile of rice from which she was removing with meticulous care bits of stones, and throwing them on the grass.'

Mahmood doesn't like his brother playing with the servants, nor are the servants' children allowed inside the family house. Shani has been crying for a bike, but Radna is delighted to have a skipping rope, which she fetches from inside the hut.

Shani stared at her. She was dressed in a coarse linen frock and had no shoes on. She wore small gold earrings, and a ring in her nose. She had long black hair, which was well oiled. A big red spot was in the centre of her forehead, which signified that she was a Hindu.

She often says, 'We each have our own dharma to fulfil.' Dad envies her inner peace.

Shani lived in a huge house surrounded by exotic trees, lush green lawns, tennis courts, rose gardens, stables and servants' quarters. His room was twice the size of their dilapidated wooden hut. Yet he was unhappy.

Ala-uddin, a fifteen-year-old kitchen boy who fancies Radna, informs Shani that he has to go and see his mother. As in 'An Indian Adolescence' she is praying, fasting, reading the Koran and organising alms for the poor.

Dad then tells this story:

One day Bibi took Shani to the Tomb of Baba, thirty miles from Poona. It was inside the courtyard of a mosque in a big white building, with a silver door. All round were trees and green fields, where horses and cows grazed, and where peacocks danced, showing off their colourful spendour, and green parrots continuously flew past screeching.

Around the marble tomb sat hundreds of pilgrims with their offerings of flowers, garlands, coconuts, fruits, sweetmeats, cloth, biryani and kebabs. In a far corner sat an old toothless man with hollow cheeks, a white flowing beard and a dirty white turban, reciting from the Koran. A small group of pilgrims sat beside him listening and chanting softly YA HU YA HU.

Here Bibi sits among the pilgrims, weeping. Dad suspects her tears are caused by the fact she has caught Colonel Murad cuddling the wife of a rich Parsi wine merchant in the back of a car.

Dad then describes the family at dinner. This is a significant scene for him, the one which has been deconstructed at the beginning of 'An Indian Adolescence', the world which in that book they are leaving behind for Bombay:

> The dining room was decorated with chandeliers, Mughal paintings, Indian brass ornaments, heavy green curtains, side tables on which were kept a vast range of silver cutlery, Wedgwood crockery, cut glasses, decanters and wine glasses. A French furniture company had made the mahogany tables and chairs, which could seat twenty-four guests.

It begins to rain; it is the start of the monsoon, and Colonel Murad, in his magnificent uniform and discussing the coming war, is about to go on manoeuvres. Niazi is present, the cousin who takes Shani to the brothel in 'An Indian Adolescence'. But this is earlier: 'He was a fierce nationalist, who had organised several strikes against the British.'

Just then a commotion breaks out. The coachman is arguing with Ala-uddin. Apparently there's a snake in the stable, which is scaring the horse that takes the two boys to school. Colonel Murad tells Niazi, who is a hunter and has killed a panther and wild boars, to go shoot the snake. But it is dark in the stable; Niazi needs someone to hold a lantern. Niazi suggests Mahmood, but Bibi refuses to let her favourite son go. Colonel Murad orders Shani to do it. 'Shani couldn't believe it. His father wanted him to hold the lantern inside the dark stable with a horse and a poisonous snake in it.' Colonel Murad leaves; dad pisses himself.

Outside the stable the Hindu servants and their relatives have gathered threateningly in the rain, bare-chested and barefoot. 'No kill snake,' they say. Niazi pushes through the crowd, pointing his rifle at them. Inside the stable with my father, Niazi shoots. The horse kicks and whines. 'His huge teeth looked like a necklace of shark's teeth.' Perhaps the snake is not dead; Shani has to get closer with the lantern. At last dad drags the dead snake out with a hockey stick.

The crowd is incensed. An old woman puts the dead snake under a tree – 'To do puja. We don't want evil spirits here.'

Did the snake see dad? In Colonel Murad's absence did the spirit of the snake enter my father? Next morning dad has a fever; all night he has been delirious. The snake, the gun and the horse, those searing symbols, won't leave him alone, and how could they? The father is absent; Bibi has to call another doctor. Nani hurries across from her part of the house and scolds Bibi for letting Shani go out in the rain.

We then learn the most significant thing, which, if it were to be true, has to change my conception of father's life. We hear that after the birth of Mahmood, Colonel Murad and Bibi's marriage had broken down and even become brutal. When Colonel Murad smashed up the house, it would take the servants hours to clear up. In an attempt to reform the marriage, Colonel Murad had taken Bibi to the hill station at Murree, in the north of India, where she'd become pregnant with my father. She tried to have an abortion but it was too late.

Colonel Murad gave Bibi a child rather than himself, a child she can only reject like an unwanted gift. Colonel Murad then returned to his old ways, buying his mistress a black MG from his poker winnings. Shani was brought up by an ayah and by Nani. He was an unwanted child – a shade therefore, belonging nowhere forever, destined always to be incurably lonely. My job, in the light of this, was to be a lifetime companion, the good brother. Maybe it was around this period that Bibi went into her room and became entirely faithful to Islam, desired only by God. Of course, in reality, she and Colonel Murad had at least three more children, though this is not mentioned.

In the light of this, the pivotal relationship of 'The Redundant Man' seems clearer to me: it is a likeness of Colonel Murad and Bibi, which dad seems to have grafted onto the London suburbs, passing his own children onto his parents for the purpose of this story. This might explain my confusion as to why the central character is so unsympathetic and unlike the way dad actually was himself. Since then I have learned that my father was 'unwanted', which I see as a kind of existential superfluity, the notion dad explores with such fury in 'The Redundant Man'. The unwanted will always feel irrelevant wherever they are and whatever they do.

It is curious, this novel written on the back of flyers for spiritual healers. One advertises a lecture series: 'Subjects include: Physical man – The Nervous and Glandular System; Healers' Conduct and the Act of Healing; The Creative Mind.' I have reviewed books before, but never the paper they were written on. Nevertheless, this helps me recall that, at the end of his life, my father became firm friends with a local faith healer. He, she and my mother would go around together and I would wonder why dad was interested in this stuff. Now I learn that Nani considers herself a sort of 'hakim, a healer, a practitioner of Ayurvedic medicine'. She would take to her bed with a red hot brick wrapped in a towel on her stomach, which would stimulate her sluggish liver. Or she'd cover herself in leeches, to purify her blood. Colonel Murad, a proper doctor, disapproved, and threw a bucket of water over her.

I have to say that my grandfather is going up in my estimation. I like his uniform and gun, his valet, his club and gambling habits, as well as his mistresses with their black MGs. His taste in green I could forfeit; otherwise, to me, he's a magnetic figure. I remember Sattoo referring to him as 'a great man'. With a whingeing son like my father, and a wife like Bibi – depressed, lost, unhappy in her room fiddling and diddling with her prayer beads, attempting, like dad later, to wrest satisfaction from religion – it isn't surprising that he is irritable and frustrated on occasions. Reading so much about him in my father's books, what I miss is seeing him as a younger man, with his other sons and daughters. I can also see now that dad was far more like his own father than he could acknowledge. Colonel Murad gave instructions and controlled the family by calling on their love and loyalty; if that failed, he'd use force. Dad didn't use force, and he was more closed, inhibited and afraid than his own father, having had the life knocked out of him early on. Dad was also kinder; he wanted to be a good father and he liked children – we were at the centre of his life. It makes me feel guilty to say it, but despite this I like Colonel Murad's authority. With my own sons, at times, I feel weak and without conviction; I have no idea how to punish them, or whether I should punish them at all. If I do lose my temper, I apologise so profusely it makes them embarrassed.

It is not, however, the saintly Nani who can make dad well. While Shani is lying ill – he may well die – the book shifts direction, successfully, in my view. He hardly ever does it, but dad is better at writing other characters, and from other points of view, than he knows.

We are in a hut in a village where the servant girl Radna's family live. Upset at Shani's condition, Radna bravely goes to

Bibi and tells her she is intending to help. Radna then fetches a Hindu holy man, Sepira. Radna understands it was the snake's gaze – seeing dad's fear and murderousness – which has poisoned Shani. In the Murad family house the Moulvi and his colleagues are preparing the last rites. Bibi, distraught, is getting ready for Shani's body to be washed and buried. We must not forget, of course, that she has lost one son already, in China.

Sepira the snake charmer is a magnificent figure before whom believers prostrate themselves 'as he passed through the narrow mean alleys with their gooey sweet shops, crowded chai restaurants, vegetable stalls, beggars, cows, naked sadhus, wrinkled old men sleeping on charpoys, bullock carts loaded to the sky with sugar canes, tongas and human excrement lying in lumps around which flies swarmed'. He has a mystical relationship with snakes and other reptiles. As he walks through Colonel Murad's house he murmurs, 'Fetters, all fetters . . .'

We regard him from Bibi's point of view:

Naked down to his feet, except for a short black loin cloth wrapped around his thin waist, he was without an ounce of fat on his jet black body. His hair was wavy and shoulder length, which he tied at the back with a red ribbon. He wore a broad red band on his forehead which almost covered the three lines of white paste on it. His beard was short and neat with a fluffy moustache woven into it.

Despite being a Muslim, Bibi lets the Hindu holy man in. Sepira massages Shani with oil. 'Suddenly he grabbed his leg and bit the vein near his ankle and sucked a little, and then quickly spat out a yellowish red streak of blood on the floor. He kept doing it with each leg until Shani's blood turned red.'

Having succeeded in saving dad by removing the poison, the Sepira meditates and chants. Under his spell, dad rests and

189

begins to recover. Bibi sends the Moulvi away. This illness, as a rejoinder to being unprotected, works well as a way of conjuring sympathy from women; later, of course, dad was ill for years.

Dad returns to school, where we learn he has been forced 'to wear a large cone-shaped hat on which was written, in bold letters, Dunce. He believes that something must be the matter with him: 'He must be bad.' What he does like is music. When an Irish nun, Sister Ursula, gives piano lessons he listens outside the door. He wants to play the piano but his father forbids it. Dad writes: 'You have observed that in our country music was played by eunuchs or Goanese cooks. It was therefore improper for a son from a martial background to waste his time.'

He seems to have a fondness for religious women; remember, he compares the prostitute in 'An Indian Adolescence' to Mother Teresa. My maternal grandmother was religious and I notice that dad's grandmother-mother-boy conjunction was replicated in our family. I was close to my grandmother; I slept in her bed, never with mother. Now, under the influence of Sister Ursula, dad begins to enjoy Bach, Handel and Irish folk songs. Another nun even puts him in her bed when he has a cold. A picture 'of a forlorn Christ on the cross' compels his attention. At home, when Bibi catches him on his knees in front of a picture of Jesus, she scolds him furiously: 'We only pray to Allah and not to false gods and idols!'

These are the consolations. Otherwise, at school, he's despised for turning up in a 'stately low black carriage, the coachman dressed in a black uniform with a white flowing turban, carrying his satchel'. What dad likes is Indian street culture: the hairdressers, dentists and hawkers. In London, my father was always fond of West Indians: for him they were noisy and uninhibited, liked music and weren't concerned about what others thought of them. The other Indian kids despise him for being too posh, as well as for his father's 'British leanings'. This causes him embarrassment with the boys who would one day run Free India. At school they carried Congress flags and stuck pictures of Gandhi and Nehru on the wall.

Despite his lack of friends, a boy in his class asks Shani to play cricket for their team, the Muslim Wanderers. Shani has already scored centuries for the Junior School XI. Even his father praised him. The game is to be played in a small village twelve miles away.

Shani has to ask Nani to take him to buy a cricket bat. The two of them go into town: in Poona dad describes the smashed-up shops; there are broken lathis, placards, banners and pamphlets all over the street, as well as fresh blood. He and Nani discuss his future. His father expects him to join the army; dad wants to be a cricketer, and Nani wants him to be a session judge.

The cricket match itself is a great scene. To my surprise, this is the first time that dad has been to an Indian village. He has only known 'westernised India'. His first sight of a leper horrifies him. Then he sees the cricket ground: 'The Maidan was a vast disused tract of land, brown in parts as it hadn't rained for weeks, and joined to a corn-field where peasants were tilling the soil. Big pats of cow dung, some fresh, others hard, lay scattered like unexploded mines all over the field.' A herd of buffaloes is driven across the pitch.

The umpire is the proprietor of the local Irani restaurant. Because he owns the cricket ball and stumps, he can insist that his fat useless son plays for the village team. When the Muslim Wanderers refuse to let the opposition win, the match is abandoned.

Seeing the village inspires an identity crisis in dad. 'Was he really an Indian?' Who are they? Shani asks Mahmood, who reads *Just William*, Sexton Blake, Sapper and Sherlock Holmes. 'How come you're more into the English than the Indian?' This, don't forget, is to the brother who later spends his life in Pakistan. Mahmood replies: '"You won't get a good job if you don't know about the English. Papa wouldn't be such a high-ranking officer if he was a Gandhiwallah." He said "Gandhiwallah" with a little contempt.'

Back at the house dad goes to see Radna, but finds her playing with Ala-uddin. Inevitably he feels excluded from them, too.

The last scene of the book is a visit from Colonel Murad's family, whom Bibi dislikes. There is an amusing incident outside the house when the family arrive – Bibi laughing at 'the big brown commode which was tied with a thick rope on the roof of the car. Karamat and his family never travelled anywhere without their private commode on which was printed in bold letters "Mr Karamat-ullah, Collector of Customs". He personally supervised what corner the commode should be put in, lest it was pointing towards Mecca.'

The book ends with dad and Shireen, his young cousin, going to the river, where dad removes his shoes and socks and lets the water run over his feet. Dad looks up and sees Radna crying. Dad realises that Shireen is the girl both families want him to marry. He sees the fate which is awaiting him. But that particular marriage is the future he refuses: it will not be his life.

*

In Pakistan Omar still has a column, 'All over the Place', and he sends me a piece he has written called 'Separate Coffins'. It is about a pair of 29-year-old Iranian twins conjoined at the head who died in Singapore after the operation to separate them failed. Omar says that no matter how terrible the world is at the moment this story touches him. He mentions that the twins wanted to be separated because one of them wanted to be a lawyer and the other a journalist. Oddly, searching for my birth certificate the other day I noticed that my father, under profession, put 'law student'. Omar, of course, was and is a journalist, born into a large family, surrounded by numerous other children, friends, servants, his grandmother and parents. Now he lives alone in a small flat in Karachi at a time when the Muslim world is in more turmoil than at any time since decolonisation.

Despite the vicissitudes of his life, Omar has written and published three autobiographical volumes, set during a fascinating period, which his family story mirrors. His books are partly about time and what it does to the idea of home. Dad often said he had no home, that he belonged nowhere, something I found hard to understand. What was 'belonging' anyway? What did it matter? Wasn't 'home' where your friends and children were? Reading the books my father and Omar wrote, I can see what 'belonging' meant in the family, and how warm and difficult and confining it might be. But my father did find another sort of belonging in the suburbs; he liked their comfort, ordinariness and lack of turmoil. When he came to see me in London, the squalid streets and the prevalence of drunks, crazies and eccentrics made him nervous. Perhaps what he wanted to escape was a memory: of intense family conflicts, religion, political turmoil.

There is no doubt, particularly in the light of Omar's third volume, *Home to Pakistan*, that the family in Pakistan lived through political chaos, corruption, violence and repression. Working in the Pakistan Embassy in London, dad was quite aware of what he was avoiding. Even Sattoo, with his business, large family, numerous friends and luxurious house in Karachi, occasionally envied dad's life in London. 'At least you know who the government is going to be tomorrow. At least you know there's going to be a government!' Omar, at the end of *Home to Pakistan*, loyal as he likes to be to the country he claims 'gave him everything', can only say, 'What has gone wrong? For something has gone wrong. It is written on the faces of the people. It is written in their eyes that something has gone wrong.' Tootoo says something to this effect when I send him a draft of this book. He writes: 'The remarks of Achoo re. the parents is not very good for the family in Pakistan where it could be bad with the mullah type thinking. Suggest you alter if you can.' He tells me that my father was the brother he loved most; dad's funeral was the worst day of his life.

Opening the green folder and reading, I discovered that my father had been writing for years about what it was like to be unwanted, and to have a more talented and favoured elder sibling. Despite this obstruction and despite much discouragement he wrote books and stories, wrote all his life, against the odds, refusing to stop speaking. I am glad I found these books of my father's; glad I read them. Father has at last received from me what he wanted when he sat down to write each morning: his stories have been read, pored over, lived with, become the subject of conversation. They've turned out, in my retelling, to mean more than he thought they meant. He'd be surprised and annoyed, amazed even, by what his work has become in my head, by how little dominion he has over the fate of his words, even as he puts his side of the story. But that is the fate of any form of expression and what happens to parents as they turn into the myths of their children.

Reading and writing my family: I think of a sixteen-year-old in a garden in Poona, leaving that Eden for Bombay, then for London and the world awaiting him; the boy who becomes the angry adult at the end of 'The Redundant Man'. Among other things, this has been a story of generations, told through the males, from my grandfather Colonel Murad/Kureishi, via my own father, his brothers, myself and my own sons, three British boys called Kureishi. Out of my reading and others' writing I have made a story of the past, imagining around their imaginations. Colonel Murad, from a military family, could seem like an authoritarian father. My own father was something of a 60s dad, wanting to be his son's friend and companion, as well as wanting to promote himself in the world through his son. And there is me, a later generation, quizzical, not knowing what a father is, what he should do, or even what a man is now. This speculation about fathers isn't only local: there is a profound relation between the sort of families that exist in a particular society – the family ideal, as it were – and the kind of political system that's possible. You couldn't have a liberal, democratic political system in a society in which the families were Muslim, strictly organised around the symbolic position of the absolute father.

Partly because of the work of the therapists and child theorists Achoo admired, children in the West are treated less harshly; there's less discipline, less emphasis on silence, good behaviour, rote learning. As well as this liberalisation, men of my generation are more likely to see the value of their lives not only in terms of financial, sexual and social success, but in terms of the sort of relationships they have had with their children. If feminism released women from the exclusive maternal function, it enabled men to reclaim that place. Being a good father means being a good mother too, and more puzzlement about the respective roles of both partners.

Apart from the political situation, I have to wonder, of course, what it might be like to live alone at Omar's age. A friend, not much younger than me, said, the other day, after his parents finally separated, 'Well, they should never have married in the first place.' And how many marriages would you say that of, that the couple could have enjoyed better lives either alone or with someone else, doing something different? In two novels dad writes about sexual passion and about the difficulty of a long marriage, that of his parents and his own. I was only a spectator at their marriage but, it seemed to me, he and mother appeared to enjoy each other's company more once the children had left home. They went to movies and museums, and travelled. Perhaps when the couple realise at last that there is no other way but acceptance and the last opportunity to find some pleasure in one another, there can be some harshly realistic assessment of what is possible.

If it seemed an effort for my parents to remember why it was they wanted to be together, there seems no doubt that the difficulties of this struggle have increased, and there is a crisis between men and women, even as relations between adults and children have altered. Most of my friends have been divorced and many of them are in 'couple therapy'. I am under no illusion that a long love will be a paradise for my children, but it is not as fatuous as the notion I was brought up to accept, in the 50s and early 60s, that each individual was destined to find their ideal, in the shape of the other, and remain with them for the rest of their life.

In the end, of course, you can never leave home. However well you know your parents, children will feel the lives of their parents are a mystery, not only because the desire and sexuality of the parents is beyond them, but because the lesson here is about unknowability. One thing you do see, though it takes a lifetime to understand it, is that a human being – your parents and then yourself – is profoundly unknowable. I have about father, after all this, the feeling you can only have after knowing someone for a long time: that you don't know them at all, really.

If only you could consign your history to the past and keep it there. But history is a blink away, the present in another aspect. And, in writing this book, I have been led to other questions, such as, what is the history of each individual? Where does it start and end, and, more importantly, how does this history continue to work in you? Unknowable though they might be, where do the dead go and what do they do? Where is my father? Ghosts take up residence within the living, of course – you can hear them speaking, the voices within – but in what way? How are these voices liberating, and how constraining? And, as time passes, how does their tone and force alter? What do they come to mean? What are the limits for the child in terms of the parent's wishes, and how does the child move beyond them? More: how is their rule from the afterlife harsher than their actual rule? To what extent do the dead determine the lives of the living? What influence do they have over them? How do you keep them vital within you? And how do you keep them out of your way in order to live within a different age, as a different person?

Father gave me what he wanted for himself, and it was a lot: for a start, the education he lacked. If I've been interested in anything it came through what was in his head, along with the daily visits to the library I made with my mother. Then, out of father's attempted writing cure, the energy of his narrow commitment, I found my own stories to tell. I cannot overestimate what a pleasure the writing life has been and how it has sustained and made me. It was where I started from and where I'm still going. Maybe, by doing this, I've given him something back; maybe the debt is done. Being a story-teller, making a living by my pen, getting the children through – father would have considered it a decent way to live, an achievement, built on a family history of which he was part.

Now, as always, I sit alone in the room waiting for a woman to come in and rescue me but no one comes. Anyhow, in the room it's okay, warm, safe, controlled; beyond, there are no maps; dad made all the maps, they belong to him, and he's taken them with him. Beyond it's chaos, wild, unknown, and that's the only place to go, to head for.

I slip dad's manuscript back into its green folder, place it under a pile of papers, and walk away, out of the room.